THOMAS MUNRO
AND THE DEVELOPMENT OF
ADMINISTRATIVE POLICY
IN MADRAS
1792–1818

THOMAS MUNRO

from the painting by M. A. Shee

THOMAS MUNRO

AND THE DEVELOPMENT OF ADMINISTRATIVE POLICY IN MADRAS

IN MADRAS

1792–1818

THE ORIGINS OF 'THE MUNRO SYSTEM'

BY

T. H. BEAGLEHOLE

Senior Lecturer in History
Victoria University of Wellington

CAMBRIDGE
AT THE UNIVERSITY PRESS
1966

PUBLISHED BY
THE SYNDICS OF THE CAMBRIDGE UNIVERSITY PRESS

Bentley House, 200 Euston Road, London, N.W. 1
American Branch: 32 East 57th Street, New York, N.Y. 10022
West African Office: P.O. Box 33, Ibadan, Nigeria

CAMBRIDGE UNIVERSITY PRESS
1966

Printed in Great Britain by
Spottiswoode, Ballantyne and Co. Ltd.
London and Colchester

LIBRARY OF CONGRESS CATALOG CARD NUMBERS: 65-17209

CONTENTS

Frontispiece

MAP

v

PREFACE

Following the great territorial acquisitions in south India made by the British at the end of the eighteenth century, a system of administration emerged in many ways markedly different from that established in Bengal. The present book is a study of how a body of ideas on administration grew up, was adopted by the home government and eventually put into effect; and more especially it deals with the part played in this process by Thomas Munro. It has long been recognised that these changes in Madras, and the development of the ryotwari system of revenue settlement, were the result of administrative ideas in contrast with those of Cornwallis which had preceded them; that they influenced subsequent administrative practice, not only in Madras, but in British India as a whole; and that in some measure Munro was responsible for the change. Although the importance of Madras and Munro has been recognised, there seems to be no full study of the way in which the ideas of the man developed, or of how far they were his alone, or of the exact manner in which they were adopted as administrative policy by the home government.

I am grateful to Dr Kenneth Ballhatchet for the advice and criticism he gave while guiding the research on which this book is based. The library staffs at the India Office Library and Record Collection, Commonwealth Relations Office, London, at the British Museum, the Nottingham University Library and the Madras Record Office were generous with their help. The frontispiece is reproduced by courtesy of the National Portrait Gallery. Mr John Saltmarsh, Mr Christopher Morris, Professor F. L. Wood and Professor J. C. Beaglehole have all been good enough to read and comment on the typescript, or early drafts of it. I am deeply indebted to King's College, Cambridge, for its abundant generosity. Cambridge University, through a subsidy from the Thirlwall Prize Fund, has assisted with the publication of this book.

T. H. B.

WELLINGTON
May 1964

Superior figures in the text refer to notes, which begin on p. 140. A glossary will be found on pp. 172–3.

INTRODUCTION

In the history of British imperial development the end of the eighteenth century and the beginning of the nineteenth was a period of renewed activity, of new objectives, altering with the great social and economic changes in Britain itself. While the 'first British Empire' was collapsing ignominiously in North America, Asia and the Pacific were the setting for a conscious revival of the Elizabethan ambition to open up new fields of commerce. The 'second British Empire' was not an empire in the old sense. The hope and intention was to open markets for the rapidly widening range of British manufactures by creating a network of commercial ports throughout the Pacific and Indian Oceans. The expense and friction attending the establishment of territorial jurisdiction were to be avoided, and with them the potential industrial competition of settlements of British colonists. It was to be an empire consisting of a chain of trading posts, inhabited, for the most part, by Asians and Africans, and ruled 'not through representative institutions, but by a strong, benevolent bureaucracy directed from London'.[1]

Such was the idea. In fact, what happened—for reasons stemming from local circumstances, the influence of interested groups, or the intractable demands of power politics—was often quite different. In India, in particular, territorial jurisdiction could not be avoided. Far from being limited to a number of trading posts, the dominions of the East India Company expanded to an extent that made the Company into the greatest power in the sub-continent. This came about largely through a series of developments which were viewed with distaste by the Directors of the Company, and strongly deplored by its numerous critics. The purpose of the present study is not to disentangle the extraordinary complexity of the forces which brought about this enormous increase in territorial control, but rather to see how (in one part of India) the power acquired was exercised. The Company's India was the scene of a complete breakdown in government machinery. The machinery had to be reconstructed. The method of reconstruction is an index to the administrative capacity of the Company and its servants. What was done and what was written alike illuminate contemporary ideas on the nature of British rule in India.

Adam Smith was one standard-bearer of the 'second British Empire'; the other was Edmund Burke. To Burke more than to any other individual person, credit is due for the genesis of the idea that with imperial control goes responsibility.

All political power which is set over men [he told the House of Commons in a debate on the powers of the East India Company] and ... all privilege claimed or exercised in exclusion of them, being wholly artificial, and for so much a derogation from the natural equality of mankind at large, ought to be some way or other exercised ultimately for their benefit. ... such rights, or privileges ... are all in the strictest sense *a trust*; and it is the very essence of every trust to be rendered *accountable*.

In the years after the suicide of Clive public opinion on the question of British rule in India was transformed: in the drawn-out acrimony of the impeachment and trial of Warren Hastings perhaps the one thing that emerged clearly was the fact that moral obligation—the motif of the speeches of Burke, Fox and Sheridan—was accepted by all, not least by Hastings himself.

The first great reforms of the Company's administrative system were those carried out by Cornwallis in Bengal. Faced with the problem of creating efficient machinery for imposing peace, dispensing justice, and restoring the Company's finances ruined by corruption and mismanagement, his solution was to break radically with the attempts of Clive and Hastings to work through the native system of administration. He effected an immediate and final settlement of the revenue with the zamindars, or hereditary rent collectors, and introduced a judicial system entirely separate from the revenue branch. The zamindars were recognised as the owners of their estates, which could be sold for arrears of revenue. A Whig idealisation of landed property was complemented by the Whig idea of reducing the executive role of government to the very minimum, of establishing the rule of law in place of what was seen as the corrupting influence of personal power. It was a policy British in origin and spirit.

Under Cornwallis, and even more under Wellesley, Fort St George was transformed from a small settlement on the east coast into the administrative capital of a great presidency which, strategically, was unchallenged in the south of India, and, territorially, stretched from coast to coast, encircling Mysore and bordering on Hyderabad and, in the west, the Maratha territories. At first the home government—that is, the Court of Directors of the East India Company, and the Board of Commissioners for the control of India which represented Parliament—and its representatives in India believed that the Bengal system of administration should be extended to these new possessions.

In the years between 1793 and 1814, however, a new idea and system of administration emerged, markedly different in many ways from that existing in Bengal. It was eventually adopted by the home government, and instructions were sent to Madras to have it put into effect. The changes, for which Thomas Munro was the foremost advocate, marked both an appreciation of and a desire to preserve the property rights and the social system found in that part of India; it marked also a reaction against the Cornwallis system, against its aim to support a British pattern of landed property by a judicial system British in spirit and largely administered by Europeans. For the home government it was a reaction which was largely caused by the growing realisation that the Company had in India an administrative structure inefficient, expensive and failing in its purpose of bringing security and justice to the Indians. Munro and his friends in Madras shared Burke's repugnance against overturning an immemorial system of society in order to promote reforms based on 'abstract theory'. They shared too the absorbed and sympathetic interest in Indian society of Warren Hastings, and with him were ready to use Indian forms of revenue and judicial administration. This was a view, essentially conservative, which went back to the earlier eighteenth century, and with it went a thoroughly paternalist view of government: not, one would have thought, a likely source for later administrative reforms. But in fact, the paternalist insistence on giving the executive arm of government a preponderant authority and prestige was the only way of alleviating the weakness inherent in the rule of law when it was applied to subject territories. This was to be accepted all over India, and, indeed, in the whole field of British colonial administration.

Cornwallis had thought otherwise. To him, power in the hands of the government, or of its servants, was fraught with grave danger: he saw the corruption and appalling mismanagement which existed in Bengal as the inevitable result of giving wide discretionary authority to underpaid and ill-controlled Company servants. The only way to prevent the abuse of power was to limit its extent. Thus he decided for 'the introduction of a new order of things, which should have for its foundation, the security of individual property, and the administration of justice, criminal and civil, by rules which were to disregard all conditions of persons, and in their operation, be free of influence or control from the government itself.'[1] The settlement of the revenue with the zamindars in perpetuity was to be as much a permanent settlement of rights as of revenue, enabling the Boards of Revenue and collectors to be stripped of all judicial powers, to act merely as collectors of revenue, under the overriding authority of the rule of law. The Cornwallis code of regulations was to be administered by the district judge and magistrate, the pre-eminent figure in the district, who was given the control of the police, and a salary and status above that of the collector.

Cornwallis realised—even if the Directors did not until later—

that in recognising the zamindars as proprietors of the soil he was going far beyond the mere recognition of existing rights, or claims acquired by prescription. To what extent the rights given to the zamindars were in fact innovations was a question in which, surprisingly, he showed little interest. While Shore and Grant, the two most eminent Bengal servants of the Company, debated whether the zamindar owned the land, and owed the state only customary revenue, or was in fact only an official acting as revenue farmer for the state which owned the land, Cornwallis wrote: 'It is immaterial to Government what individual possesses the land, provided he cultivates it, protects the ryot, and pays the public revenue.'[1] The question had been settled, though not answered, by the instructions of the Court of Directors who, following the act of parliament in 1784 which required them to establish 'permanent rules' for collecting the land revenue 'according to the laws and constitution of India', had instructed Cornwallis to make the settlement with the zamindars. The permanent settlement was seen by many as a measure 'which was effected to naturalize the landed institutions of England among the natives of Bengal';[2] without pretence that such institutions were already there, awaiting recognition. In fact Cornwallis had no alternative to a settlement with the zamindars.[3] Limited as his government service was in numbers and administrative ability he had not the means of collecting the revenue directly from the ryots. The zamindar was indispensable. It is in his conception of the rule of law securing absolutely, through its inherent principles, individual property rights, rather than in the choice of a particular landholding class, that Cornwallis's conscious and deliberate policy of anglicisation is clear—a policy which stemmed not from ignorance of Indian institutions, but perhaps from an exaggerated respect for those of England.

Cornwallis planned to give the ryots the same security of tenure in relation to the zamindars as the zamindars had in relation to the government. But the regulations drawn up for this purpose were a failure. The rights of the ryots were intended to be upheld by the courts administering the judicial code, but this the courts proved incapable of doing. Even if the reasons for their incapacity were a consequence not of any defect in the courts themselves, but rather of other circumstances—which seems to have been partly so—it did not alter the fact that Cornwallis's faith that they could protect the people against officials, and the ryots against the zamindars, was unjustified: the protection existed in theory alone. A great wave of litigation which followed the settlement threatened to overwhelm the judicial system completely, and the consequent delays in hearing suits led to such an accumulation of causes that application to the courts, for many, became synonymous with avoiding any legal decision. In undermining the interests of the ryots, and exalting those of the zamindars, the permanent settlement had lasting social results, wholly altering the balance of rural society in Bengal.

With Cornwallis's respect for English institutions went a belief both in the superior abilities of English officials, and in the necessity, if the security of the Company's position was to be upheld, of having an adequate number of them. 'I think it must be universally admitted', he wrote to the Court of Directors, 'that without a large and well-regulated body of Europeans, our hold on these valuable dominions must be very insecure';[1] and while the result of his policy was to raise the standard of those European servants it also ensured that Indians were, in fact, excluded from responsible employment. This aggravated what was probably the worst result of Cornwallis's measures of 1793; the great extent to which the rulers of Bengal lost touch with the people under their charge.

Both Henry Dundas, the President of the Board of Control, and Wellesley in India were convinced that the Bengal methods should be extended to every region under the Company's authority, and in 1798 Wellesley sent instructions to Madras for the introduction of revenue and judicial arrangements modelled on those of Bengal. This action the Court of Directors wished to condemn,[2] their disapproval stemming not so much from disagreement with the basis of the policy—in spite of the fact that the land tenures of south India differed fundamentally from those in Bengal and in only a few regions of Madras was there a zamindari class—as from a wish to avoid a permanent settlement while 'the real value of the land in many cases [was] very imperfectly known'; and above all because in this field, as in every other, they felt Wellesley was gathering to himself power and authority which, in their opinion, should emanate from them.[1] Dundas strongly supported Wellesley and wished to allow him to act on his own initiative, and the Directors reluctantly gave way.[2]

As zamindars were virtually non-existent, the Madras Board of Revenue proposed that villages should be grouped to form estates of convenient size to be sold by auction to the highest bidders, and a settlement on these lines was begun in the districts of Baramahal, Dindigul and the Northern Circars.[3] During 1802 the introduction of the judicial system was begun in those districts that had been permanently settled, and by 1806 the courts had been established even outside the permanently settled areas of the presidency. In 1802, however, Henry Dundas left the Board (where he was succeeded by Castlereagh) and the Court in a despatch ordered that in those districts where the settlement had not been made its conclusion should be suspended until the Madras government were able to find out whether all possible information had been obtained on the real value of their resources, and until this had been specifically reported to the Court with the relevant information.[4] This order was repeated several times in subsequent despatches,[5] but reflected an anxiety not to forgo undiscovered sources of revenue rather than doubts as to the suitability of the system. A 'permanent settlement' was still automatically taken to mean a zamindari settlement—though the Court did receive reports of 'individual proprietary rights' in parts of the presidency, and enjoined great caution in applying the settlement to such districts.[6]

In Madras there was a growing opinion that the Cornwallis

system was not suited to those territories. Many of the proprietors of the newly created estates began to fall into arrears. By 1806, many of the estates were sold, and when such alienated estates lapsed into the direct management of government, it was discovered that the prosperity of most of the villages had deteriorated under the exactions of the late proprietors. Support grew for a ryotwari settlement, a plan first developed by Alexander Read in the Baramahal between 1792 and 1799, and applied, apparently with striking success, by Thomas Munro during his administration of the Ceded Districts from 1801 to 1807. The ryotwari settlement was based on a permanent assessment of the rent to be paid on each field, to be decided following a general survey of all the land, and an annual agreement between each cultivator or ryot and the government, which recorded how much land he cultivated that year. It was a system which brought the collector into close and continual contact with the mass of the people, which needed a large number of native administrative officers to make it work, and was, in some respects, incompatible with the Bengal judicial system. In common with the Cornwallis system it sought to establish individual proprietary rights in land, but the proprietors envisaged were very different. 'Supposing the amount of property to be the same', wrote Munro, 'it would be better that it should be in the hands of forty or fifty thousand small proprietors, than four or five hundred great ones';[1] and this he held was true both because of the beneficial effect on the revenue, and as a socially desirable end.

Between the two systems there was much more than simply a preference for small cultivators over great landowners. By dividing power and giving the first place to the judicial arm of administration Cornwallis sought to protect the people from the government. In the Madras system the object was the protection of the community by, and not against, the government; and for this purpose it was held, in general, that the more power bestowed upon the collector the more effective he could be at this task.

If asked what the community needed protection from, Munro

and his school would probably have used the terms 'innovation' or 'regulation'.

It is too much regulation that ruins everything; Englishmen are as great fanatics in politics as Mahomedans in religion. They suppose that no country can be saved without English institutions. The natives of this country have enough of their own to answer every useful object of internal administration, and if we maintain and protect them, our work will be easy. If not disturbed by innovation, the country will in a very few months settle itself.[1]

The ryotwari plan was strongly supported by the governor of Madras, Lord William Cavendish Bentinck,[2] who went so far as to travel to Calcutta to impress his argument on the supreme government.[3] Under him several districts were settled on the ryotwari principle and detailed reports on its progress sent home. Following the Vellore mutiny in 1807 Bentinck was recalled, and the despatch to Madras communicating the resolution of recall was more than a condemnation of his failure to avoid the mutiny, being rather 'a general censure on the conduct of the latter part of his Government'. Bentinck's attitude to the permanent settlement, according to Auber, was one of the grounds of disapprobation; 'but', he wrote, 'it was a question upon which party feeling prevailed, and his Lordship's views were as strongly supported a short time afterwards, as they had been previously disapproved'.[4]

It was probably the mutiny rather than the actual minutes, reports and letters on administration which brought the nature of the administrative system into discussion. The 'Saints' among the Directors were determined to find causes other than religious ones for the mutiny, and in May 1807 the 'Chairs',[5] in a letter to the President of the Board, suggested that much of the unrest in Madras had been caused by the exclusion of Indians from the more important government posts which had followed the extension of the Bengal system to that Presidency.[6] Even before the mutiny Charles Grant, in a private letter to Bentinck, had written agreeing that the Bengal zamindari settlement, in spite of the efforts made to protect the ryots from the oppression of the 'corrupt & faithless

Zemindar', had not secured the 'comfort & the industrious exertion of the body of the people'; and Grant appears to have accepted Bentinck's arguments in favour of a ryotwari settlement.[1] This critical attitude did not lead the Directors generally to support the ryotwari plan, and in August 1809, having received a report of Munro's on the method of making a ryotwari settlement, they wrote that while they believed the ryotwari system 'intelligently followed up . . . well calculated to discover the resources of a country, yet we also think that after it has answered that end, it is not to be preferred for constant practice'.[2]

In the six years following Munro's return to Britain on leave in 1808, the Court of Directors, urged on by the Board of Control, changed its mind, and accepted first the ryotwari system, and then the ideas of judicial reform that went with it.[3] Munro returned to India as Special Commissioner to revise the Madras judicial system, and he was instructed as well to make recommendations on revenue matters. By his contemporaries, Elphinstone and Metcalfe among them, and by his successors, the reforms he made and the administrative system he established at this time and while he was Governor of Madras (1820–7), were always known as the 'Munro system'. The name was not undeserved.

In considering how the 'Munro system' became administrative policy in Madras, and influenced policy in the rest of British India, there are a number of questions that must clearly be distinguished. Though the system marked a reaction against that of Cornwallis, the reaction was one which, for Munro and those of his contemporaries at Madras who shared his views, was the result more of the study of the institutions of their part of India than of any theoretical objections to the Bengal system. The introduction of this into parts of the Madras presidency had led to the deprivation of existing property rights, and to the impoverishment of many districts. These discouraging results both drew attention to the differences in land tenures and revenue practice between Madras and Bengal, and demonstrated weaknesses in the judicial system, which while they were also becoming apparent in Bengal, had scarcely come to the attention of the home government. Therefore Munro's ideas largely resulted from what he observed in Madras— though one must not fail to remember that what he noticed was to some extent determined by his character and preconceptions. But it does not follow that those ideas were adopted by the home government for exactly the same reasons. In England the question was conceived much more in terms of the Cornwallis system and its results, and was complicated because the extraordinary and almost universal veneration for Cornwallis's character for some years seemed to inhibit any critical assessment of his work.

CHAPTER I

MUNRO AND READ IN THE
BARAMAHAL, 1792–9

For Cornwallis, Tipu's ambition to win supremacy in the south of India had international implications. The Governor-General saw India as a vital point in the international rivalry between England and France, and in March 1788 he wrote, 'I look upon a rupture with Tipu as a certain and immediate consequence of a war with France, and in that event a vigorous co-operation of the Marathas would certainly be of the utmost importance to our interests in this country.'[1] The actual outbreak of hostilities followed Tipu's attack on Travancore on 29 December 1789; in June and July following, treaties were made with the Marathas and the Nizam, both of whom were in greater fear of Tipu than of the English, and after delays caused by the breath-taking incompetence and corruption of the Madras government, the war finally began. It was to last two years and to bring disaster to Tipu. In 1791 Cornwallis himself took command and in February 1792 Tipu was driven back to his capital, Seringapatam. Cornwallis had no desire to crush his enemy completely, and was urged by his native allies to negotiate a peace. By the treaty of Seringapatam, 16 March 1792, Tipu surrendered half his territory, a large portion of it to the Nizam and the Marathas. The raja of Coorg was given independence, and the East India Company secured all Tipu's lands on the Malabar coast between Travancore and the Kaway, the district of Dindigul and that of the Baramahal.

The Baramahal was a district about 140 miles in length, with an average width of 60 miles. Salem, the principal town of the district, was a centre of extensive commerce, all the overland traffic between Malabar and the eastern coast, north and south from

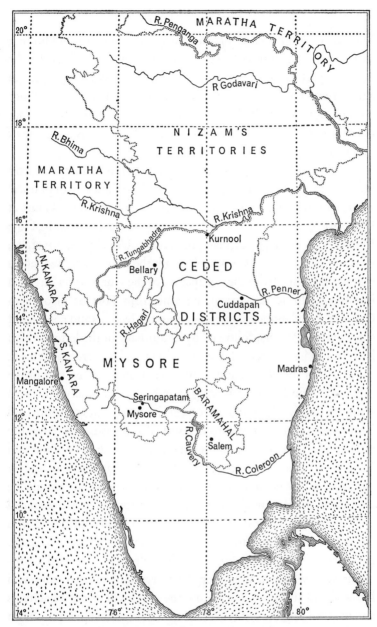

Map showing the territories under the government of Fort St George in which Munro was stationed. The Baramahal became the Salem collectorate; the Ceded Districts were divided into Bellary, Cuddapah and part of Kurnool.

Madras to Pondicherry, passing through it, while in addition a large amount of cloth was manufactured in Salem itself. By far the greatest part of the population, however, was employed in agriculture, the peasants attaining little more than a subsistence level of cultivation. This district was placed by Cornwallis under the charge of Captain Alexander Read and three assistants, one of them Thomas Munro.

Read had been appointed a cadet in the Madras Infantry in 1770.[1] He mastered Persian early, devoted himself to the study of political affairs and in 1786 carried out some negotiations with the Court at Hyderabad, reporting on the armies of the Nizam and of the Marathas. Some two years later he was consulted by the governor, General Sir Archibald Campbell, about the political consequences that would ensue from the occupation of the Guntoor Sirkar, then imminent. In January 1789, he sent from Fort St George to Campbell an elaborate statement about the feelings and conduct of the Country Powers, followed by a summary of the letters which he seems to have received almost daily from his correspondents at the courts of the Nizam and Tipu. Accordingly when war broke out with Tipu in the following year he was naturally entrusted with the duties of intelligence officer, in control of transport, and it was at this time that Munro first served as his assistant. After the peace of Seringapatam, and his experience in charge of Kolar and Bangalore when they were temporarily occupied, it was equally natural that, in default of any competent civilian, he should be appointed to administer the annexed territory of the Baramahal and Salem. It was natural, because although Read's 'principle' was 'to exert himself, and to leave it to Government to discover the necessity of employing him',[2] he had already impressed Cornwallis, with whom he was in regular correspondence, not only with his 'zeal and ability in conciliating the good will of the inhabitants and in arranging the settlements of the Districts that [had] . . . been placed under [his] . . . management', but also with his integrity, which, Cornwallis was persuaded, would make him incapable of 'attempting to obtain the smallest emolument beyond that which is open and allowed'.[1] In a letter to his father, Munro wrote of the same qualities: of a 'master, whose conduct is invariably regulated by private honour and the public interest', who had given up many of the perquisites of military command, and under whom, whatever Munro might have done had he been left to himself, he could 'get no pickings'.[2] To an 'unwearied zeal in whatever he undertakes' Read joined 'an intimate knowledge of the languages and manners of the people, and a happy talent for the investigation of everything connected with revenue'. His knowledge was coupled with a liberal disposition which made 'every allowance for the prejudices' and accommodated itself 'to the manners and customs of the people'.[3]

At the time of his appointment as one of Read's assistants Munro had been twelve years in India. Born on 27 May 1761, the second son of Alexander Munro, a Glasgow merchant trading with Virginia, and his wife Margaret Stark, Munro was well educated and was originally intended to follow his father's career. This plan had to be abandoned when, as a result of the American war, Alexander Munro's business collapsed, and it was decided that Thomas must go to India and there make his own fortune. Through the good offices of Laurence Sullivan, a Director of the East India Company and an acquaintance of Alexander Munro, a cadetship in the Company's Madras army was obtained for him, and on 15 January 1780 he landed through the surf at Fort St George.

Within a few months of his arrival he was involved in the operations against Haidar Ali led by Sir Eyre Coote and Sir Hector Munro. He early attracted the notice of Coote, and was made quartermaster of a brigade when still an officer of less than two years' service. In August 1788, he was appointed an assistant in the Intelligence Department, where he first came under Alexander Read, and he served throughout the campaign against Tipu, though he missed the final attack on Seringapatam. His letters home at this time show a forthright and clear mind, with little sympathy for the incompetence he saw around him, and no hesitancy in advocating great plans of conquest.

There are times and situations [he wrote to his father] where conquest not only brings a revenue greatly beyond its expenses, but brings also additional security. . . . while [Tipu's] power remains unimpaired, so far from being able to extend our territory, we shall be perpetually in danger of losing what we have. Why not remove, while we can, so formidable an enemy? [1]

Lieutenant Munro's advice however was not asked. Cornwallis negotiated a peace, by which Tipu 'lost half his revenue . . . [but] by no means . . . half his power',[2] and the British army broke up, the several divisions each returning to its own presidency. At this point, apart from two short periods, Munro's active military career came to an end. The grave shortage of competent civilian servants, as well as the qualities he had already shown, led to his selection to serve under Read in the administration of the Baramahal.

The immediate problem before Read and his assistants was to restore the Baramahal to peace and order and take up the age-old function of any Indian government—the assessment and collection of the land revenue. In theory Read was under the Board of Revenue at Fort St George;[3] in practice, his distance from Fort St George, as well as his readiness blandly to ignore the Board when he wished to, meant that for seven years the policy followed was very much his own. In drafting regulations and establishing a method of collecting the revenue Read was much more concerned to persuade Munro and his other assistants of the justice and practicability of his plans than he was to convince and carry with him his superiors on the Board.

Read fixed the date of the peace treaty, March 1792, as the period from which the revenue should be collected by the English, and in June of that year proposed a lease-settlement for not less than five years. In November the Board of Revenue instructed him to make a settlement with the cultivators for from three to five years; and they further intimated that if the headmen of villages should oppose these measures the land might be let out in small portions to strangers.[1] Having concluded that five years would give sufficient time for a survey and assessment of the arable lands to be completed, the government decided in the next month that the lease should be for that period. This was viewed as the necessary preliminary to a permanent settlement, from which great benefits were expected.

A thousand advantages must result from a plan of permanency [the Board of Revenue recorded] not only by exciting the people to improvements, but by enabling government to effect a reduction of the revenue officers . . . by reducing in general the charges of collection; by ensuring regular payments; by rendering the revenue accounts more simple; and, above all, by putting a stop to intrigue and corrupt practices.[2]

A lease for five years would provide a period in which 'every necessary information ought to be obtained relative to the value and state of the country'. After this a settlement on the principles of that in Bengal, principles which were, in the Board's opinion, 'so excellent that [they] may be safely taken as a model on this coast', should be made.[3]

The settlement in lease having been decided on, Read and his assistants began an exhaustive enquiry into the 'nature and progress of agriculture'—this, Read declared, being the 'surest means of ascertaining an equitable mode of assessment and collection of the land rent'.[4] The results of the enquiry were communicated to the Governor-General in Read's 'fifth report' of 1 July 1793.[5] In the preceding month he had written to the President of the Board of Revenue explaining his report and drawing various conclusions from it.[6] After discussing various kinds of revenue management he rendered his opinion in favour of 'giving villages or divisions of districts in . . . perpetual management to their present farmers, and to *tax their rents* a certain proportion which would be the same as allowing them a commission upon their collection.'[7] The farmers would let out plots to the greatest advantage, and by a 'rigorous administration of justice' the government would protect the rights of the tenants. The question of the size of these farms is discussed by Read in general terms with little reference to existing practice.[1] Small farms should have the advantage, he wrote, of raising the 'bulk of the inhabitants from extreme indigence to comfort', by promoting industry through the wide distribution of the profits of farming. But the extreme poverty of the cultivators, their vulnerability to complete failure in poor seasons, meant that their holding the lands individually, and immediately of government, 'would be detrimental to cultivation, and make revenue precarious'.[2] 'The arguments in favour of improvements and the certainty of revenue are . . . in favour of giving a number of villages in farm to wealthy individuals with security; for having stock at command, they could enter into more extensive undertakings, and make up for losses sustained in one or more whole villages by their profits on others.'[3] Here Read is echoing the case then being made in Bengal in favour of a zamindari settlement, while at the same time being aware of the objections to depriving the bulk of the peasantry of the profits of farming and of keeping them in a state of dependence. Read concludes,

the greater the division of the country into farms, the more beneficial to the commonalty and favourable to the population; and the larger the farms are, to a certain extent, the more certain the increase of cultivation and the receipts of revenue. The assigning whole villages individually, or in number, to the most responsible of their present tenants, giving each a grant of his farm or estate for the time of the lease, on condition of paying the rent that may be regulated by the present valuation, binding each to be separately answerable for the payment of their own rents, and jointly so, for the payment of the whole revenue of their corporation, is a mode that has occurred as the best for combining all advantages to the inhabitants in general and to revenue.[4]

Read believed that the actual method advocated by him for assessing the rent was evolved directly from the indigenous system which he found in the Baramahal.[5] First he ascertained from the village records the gross revenue as settled by Tipu at the time when his revenue was greatest, and then his own collections in the preceding year. Then he checked the ryots' estimates of the produce with those of his own officers. He checked them also with the offers made by the patels and others who came to bid for the leases of those districts which, according to the Board of Revenue's decision, were offered to the highest bidder, for a period of five years, in return for the regular collection of the revenue for the government. From this examination Read formed an estimate of what each district was worth, and determined that 94 per cent of Tipu's revenue might be taken as the standard assessment. The rent was to be paid in money and was equivalent, Read believed, to half the gross produce in an average year.[1] Although calculated from the produce, the rent, Read maintained, must at some time have been 'fixed to the soil . . . for every plot has a standard rent, which the inhabitants affirm never alters',[2] though it had in fact been usual 'to correct the assessment annually by those of preceding years, and to ascertain, as far as practicable, the Amildars' collections by investigations of the village registers'.[3] Read concluded that

a settlement in lease could not be fixed on particular productions or the crops, nor accommodated to particular castes or occupations although done in annual assessments because of their continual change, therefore, that it must be fixed on the soil. It being usual to grow several kinds yielding very unequal profit in the same soil and impracticable to rear the most beneficial every year, suggested the laying it down as one principle, that the rent of land should be regulated by the average produce of the kinds they grow.[4]

In a letter to Read, 31 July 1793,[5] Munro gave his views on the report. Read, he wrote, had almost convinced him that he had 'discovered a set of general infallible rules for regulating a land tax'. But admitting the truth of all Read's principles and 'even of [his] calculations with a few exceptions . . . there is still after all a great impediment to the progress of the survey in the difficulty of carrying the principles into practice, because a tedious investigation of the produce and expense of labour etc. in every district must always precede their application'.[6] He agreed that to fix the rent upon the soil was 'the best mode of any', but feared that the prevalence of unequal assessment of different castes would make it difficult to accomplish. In spite of the fact, Munro wrote, that no 'investigation of revenue affairs so minute, so correct and so original ... [had] ever been made by any European in India', the information was so badly arranged that 'it would be idle ... to suppose that the heads of Revenue Board men will comprehend one half' of it. This stricture was fully justified; as one of his successors in the Baramahal has written, Read indeed 'sadly wanted that perspicuity of style which was so essential for an office that he held otherwise so worthily'.[1] The freedom with which Munro made his criticisms bears witness to the admirable relations between the two men. Having discussed various details, Munro continued:

I have now done with you as a Collector and shall just let fly one volley at you as a politician.

Talking of the contingency you say, you will endeavour to ascertain what is the smallest sum that will answer this end in order that nothing may be lost to revenue. This is the language of a tax gatherer, not of a politician. Revenue ought not to be all that the subject can pay but only what the necessities of the state require ... it is neither wise nor just to demand more, the remainder will be more beneficial to the country in the hands of the subject than in the treasury of Government.[2]

Munro's aversion to viewing the collector simply as a tax gatherer, which is here first expressed, remained strong throughout his career. He is ready, and has the vision, to view administration as something much more comprehensive.

The revenue settlement for the first year had been made with the heads of villages, and while it brought to the village patels the benefits of farming which had previously been enjoyed only by those controlling large tracts of country—generally to the detriment of those under them—it was found that 'great abuses still prevailed by the patels ... being able to evade payments of their own rents, favour their friends, and make extra collections from the rest of the ryots not only on account of the public revenue but for many private purposes.'[1] However Read, who had come to the job with a strong sympathy for the ryot,[2] decided in the second year to extend the division of landed property to include ryots below the village patels among those who held land immediately from government. By this means, he believed, they would be 'advanced from a state of dependent servitude, and extreme poverty, to be the proprietors of their own farms, and to be more immediately under the collector's protection'.[3] A survey was an essential basis of such a plan, and by the middle of 1794 Read and his assistants had surveyed the greater part of the districts assigned to them. In a letter to Read, Munro described his way of making the settlement:

The value of the land of every man who paid a single rupee of rent was ascertained as nearly as time would permit, a patta signed by me was given to him individually specifying the quantity and nature of his ground, and the rent to be paid, and from the amount of these pattas was formed the assessment of the village for which a patta containing a list of the rents and names of the ryots was given to the patel but he was expected to act merely as a Collector of rents for he had no authority either to raise or diminish them in any instance; a small piece of ground was given to him at a low valuation for the trouble he had in executing the duties of his station.[4]

This 'emancipation of petty farmers from the control of intermediate ones'[5] meant that each of the three divisions of the collectorate contained over twenty thousand renters,[6] the 'greatest part of whom', according to Munro, had always been 'accustomed to be plundered by their Gours, in league with an army of revenue officers under the Mysore Government'.[7] The submission of the population in face of private levies made the discovery of such levies the 'most difficult part of the collector's business', and Munro believed that the Brahmans of the different kachahri, in the districts under Read, collected privately 'above fifty thousand rupees a year for favouring certain individuals in the valuation of their lands at their annual settlements',[8] which in fact caused a loss to revenue of more than twice that sum because of the decrease in rents thus obtained, and because the ryots would save money to bribe the Brahmans which ought to have been used for increasing cultivation. The only effectual way of putting an end to such abuses, on which Read, Munro and the Board of Revenue were at this time in full agreement, was the institution of long leases following the completion of the survey, of making everything as 'distinct, simple, and permanent as possible'.[1]

By the lease [wrote Munro] every man will become sole master of his own land; when he pays his rent there will be no further claims against him. . . . the collection of the revenue will become easy and regular, and the present shameful system . . . of a continual struggle between the inhabitants to elude, and the collector to enforce payment, will be done away.[2]

After the experience of the first year's collection Read was led to make a change also in the method of realising the settlement. It had at first been laid down that the patels of whole tahsildaries or large portions of districts should be individually and jointly answerable for the amount of the rents; that if one village loss was so great as to be beyond the capacity of its members to make it good, then the joint obligation should be extended from one village to five or six. Only in this way, Read believed, could a permanent revenue to government be ensured.[3] Munro saw 'such objections' to carrying this system of obligation to 'its utmost extent' that, he wrote, it 'would be better to limit [it] to narrower bounds', to a village or villages with a rent of about 500 pagodas, 'because within so narrow a circle ryots are acquainted with each others circumstances, they see at once what means there are of answering the claims of the sarkar—and they are not deterred by the apprehension of unforeseen losses coming upon them from a distant quarter from exerting themselves in improving their lands'.[4] Read came to the same conclusion, and reported to the Board of Revenue that the joint securities were mostly 'limited to the petty farmers of single villages who . . . must know, when there really is a failure . . . and can best judge of the ability [to pay] of every individual of their number'.[5]

The Board accepted Read's report[1] and orders were issued that the annual settlement of 1794 should be upheld until the conclusion of the survey and the permanent settlement of the districts in lease. By the middle of 1795, however, Read was coming to the conclusion that a lease settlement was impracticable in the district since the share taken by the state was so large, and favourable terms to the ryots were essential for lease settlements to be successful. There was, Read believed, 'in fact nothing left to the cultivators from which might be created the capital absolutely requisite for a strict adherence to such engagements'.[2] This was a difficulty which Munro, at first, refused to see. He questioned Read's estimate that the government demanded one-half of the produce as revenue, giving his view that it was 'not on an average more than one third'.[3] The poverty of the ryots[4] he attributed not to the actual assessed revenue—nor, it is worth noting, to the 'idleness' of the ryots, or to 'the sun'—but to the 'violent ... manner of making the collections and to the arbitrary system of exacting fines under the old Government'. This, he wrote to Read, 'was carried to such a length that there was hardly a single rayet above the poorest class who did not under Tippoo pay more in fines than in rent—and a man was often deprived at once of all that he had saved himself and inherited from his father'.[5] About the remedy he was quite clear: 'we have only to guard the Ryots from oppression, and they will create the revenue for us'.[6] It would take time and patience, and a security for the ryot which could only be achieved when the land was made over 'either in very long lease, or in perpetuity', to its occupants.[7]

Read's alternative to the settlement of districts in lease was outlined in the circular he drew up, dated 10 December 1796, explaining to the ryots of his district the rules for making the revenue settlement.[8] Following the survey, the assessment of every individual field was to be fixed for ever.

Government [it was laid down] is never to require more or receive less ... unless when those fields actually dry shall hereafter be converted into wet by the construction of tanks, etc., at the expense of Government, when the rates will be proportionately raised according to the consequent increase of the produce and in like manner fixed for ever. But if you carry on such works at your own expense ... you may depend on receiving the advantages accruing from these, and from every other improvement of your land while you continue to pay the established rates; those constituting except in the case above mentioned, the annual demand upon them on the part of the Circar for ever.

The great change from the idea of a lease by which the tenant agreed to pay the revenue of a particular area for a set number of years was the provision for 'annual tenants', who entered into an obligation for one year only (and only for the fields they themselves cultivated) but were allowed to occupy the same fields the year following and so long as they should continue to pay regularly the established rent of them. They were free to 'extend or reduce their farms according to their circumstances, by retaining or rejecting certain fields, as they [chose] from year to year'. Read also provided for 'leaseholders', who

from thinking it will add to the security of their possession, or desiring to avoid the trouble of annual stipulations, shall desire to have puttahs for the whole, or for part of their land, in lease for a term of years, [and] will in like manner be allowed the privilege of occupying them, while they continue to pay regularly the established rent.

Read sent the rules, before publishing them, to his assistants for their views, and Munro wrote a long and critical letter in reply.[1] Not surprisingly, in view of his advocacy of long leases, Munro strongly criticised the provision for annual changes in the extent of land a ryot might cultivate, on the grounds that it would 'discourage long tenures and cannot, therefore, be expected to produce any good effects. 'After the farmers understand it perfectly', he continued, 'they will prefer annual leases to those of a longer date, because they give them the same security and advantages, without hindering them from throwing up their lands whenever they can get a better bargain anywhere else.'[2] The objection to the expediency of the lease, that many of the ryots had failed, might be made with the same force against annual settlements: the cause of the failures could not be speedily removed, for it lay in the 'universal poverty of the farmers'.[1] He recommended a reduction of 20 per cent in the assessment of all lands, and suggested that such a reduction, besides simplifying the collection and rendering unnecessary Read's 'complicated details of changeably-rated lands', would lead to such an extension of cultivation that in ten or fifteen years revenue would probably be as much as it would have been had no abatement ever been granted. Finally he advocated making the land over in perpetuity to its present occupants, as leases for five or ten years did not provide security enough for the lands to become saleable, and 'until they shall be saleable, cultivation will never be carried to any high point of perfection, nor will revenue be permanent'.[2] Without apparently fully realising it, Munro in this last paragraph comes very close to taking up Read's position. They were agreed that a permanent money assessment should be fixed on each field—though Munro thought that Read had not been explicit enough on the permanency in his proclamation—and that the land should in fact be made over to its occupants outright provided they paid the revenue. Where Munro could not agree was in giving the ryot freedom to throw up or take on new fields annually and to be liable for revenue only on those which he was currently cultivating.

Before they left the Baramahal Munro had come round to the views of Read. In a letter to Read of 18 July 1797,[3] he began by stating that the recommendation he had made of a reduction of 20 per cent in the assessment had been made on the supposition that all the lands at that time in the lease settlement were to be kept in cultivation, but that if the ryots were to be free to give up as much of their land as they chose, thereby increasing the proportion of stock to cultivation, the saving they would make would equal the proposed reduction, which would therefore not be necessary. He had already given his 'preference to a lease on a reduced rent', he wrote, but he went on to suggest various rules that, if annual settlements were to be adopted, would 'afford to the ryots every advantage that could be granted to them, consistent with the insuring of a future permanent revenue'.[1] These rules closely followed the main ideas of Read's proclamation—though greatly simplifying its details—with changes on two points. In his seventh rule Read had provided that the land of those castes who did not till the soil should be assessed at a lower rate. Previously Munro had criticised Read for an unrealistic estimate of what Brahmans actually paid in revenue but had not objected to the principle of the rule.[2] Now, however, he wrote that 'all castes . . . should pay the same rents for the same land'. Were rents so high as to require an 'extraordinary exertion of industry' to pay them, he argued, 'a few particular castes might have claim to some indulgence'. But failures in the district were generally the result of want of stock rather than of personal labour, and this being so there seemed no reason why a Brahman, who could 'perform every operation of agricultural labour except that of holding the plough', should pay less than a ryot.[3]

The other important change from Read's proclamation was Munro's provision that 'lands . . . being given up and allowed to lie waste, no matter how many years, should when again occupied, pay the very first year the full rent as before'.[4] One of Munro's strongest objections to Read's proposal that the ryots should be free to take extra land or give up some each year had been that with the accompanying rule that waste brought into cultivation should pay a reduced rent for the first two years, the ryots would be encouraged not only to cultivate the waste but to stop cultivating their arable lands. The result would be confusion among the accounts, a lower revenue to government and none of the advantages to the ryot of long-term tenure and cultivation.[5]

By insisting always on the full rent [he now wrote], there is no danger of checking the extension of cultivation. There are few fields which, after having been long suffered to lie waste, may not in two years be rendered as productive as ever; and

26

the ryot who is in a condition to occupy highly-assessed lands, will not be deterred from it by any trifling loss which he may sustain the first year.[1]

In spite of having begun by stating his preference for a lease system Munro concludes by giving an enthusiastic description of the effects of putting Read's ideas into practice:

Revenue having reached its lowest point of depression, will, after next year, begin to rise regularly and uniformly; the ryots having changed every field that they wish to get rid of, and having chosen such as they like, will consider their farms as inalienable property, and will begin in earnest to improve them with their whole means; revenue will be permanent. . . . All the effects of a lease will thus be naturally produced, though under a different name; and the system is so simple, and the rules so few, that it may be easily managed by any collector who bestows on it the most common degree of attention.[2]

In answer to a circular from Read asking for his assistants' views on the final form of settlement to be introduced on the completion of the survey [3] Munro, after a general survey of the districts under his charge, so developed several of his arguments that he came to agree on all the main points proposed by Read. He returned to the question of the effect on the revenue of allowing the ryots to throw up land if they so wished, and decided that in spite of this freedom, nearly the same amount of land would be cultivated each successive year. There would, besides, be a saving of much expense and labour which, formerly being spent on the investigation of losses in poor seasons, would now, he believed, not occur, as the ryots by curtailing the extent of their cultivation would save 'in the natural way'. In spite of the liberty to throw up land, he held the lands to be still under-stocked, and although not doubting that the rents on all the lands occupied at that time could be collected without remission, he wrote that 'such important benefits will immediately accrue to the country, and at a future period to revenue itself, from facilitating the means of increasing the stock of the farmers', that he thought 'it would be doing an injury to both not to remit fifteen per cent of the lease assessment'.[4] Another result of the reduction would be to increase the number of farmers by encouraging labourers to take up land on their own account. In his preference for small farmers Munro agreed with Read. Great proprietors, he held, would contribute nothing to the security of the revenue, 'for they are as likely as the petty farmers to fail, from misfortune or imprudence, and more likely to do so from design; for they are more capable of intriguing and combining together, in unfavourable seasons and times of hostility, for withholding their rents, under various pretexts'.[1] Where the failure of a small farmer resulted only in a small loss to revenue, the failure of a great farmer would not only cause a loss to the government but was also likely to ruin the cultivators under him. To enable a few large farmers to bear the risk and expense of collection, the remission which would have to be made in their favour on the original assessment would far exceed the cost of the direct collection of the revenue by the officers of government. Small farms he held to be 'better on every account'; they lessened 'the number of poor' and raised up everywhere

a crowd of men of small, but of independent property, who, when they are certain that they will themselves enjoy the benefits of every extraordinary exertion of labour work with a spirit of activity which would in vain be expected from the tenants or servants of great landholders. If the expenses of collection be somewhat increased by the smallness of farms, it is amply repaid by the augmentation of revenue. . . . Were there any necessity for making great farmers, it could only be done by wronging all the petty farmers and diminishing revenue.[2]

Munro finally concludes by giving his 'opinion as to the best mode of forming a permanent settlement of the revenue of the country'.

The great point in making a settlement is the rate of assessment; all other regulations connected with it are of very inferior importance. . . . I have proposed such an abatement as, when the cheapness of cultivation and the great returns from the seed are taken into consideration, will be found to leave them in possession of as great advantages as any race of husbandmen in the world. It must not, however, from this be inferred that land will become saleable on a sudden; for the frontier situation of these districts, and other reasons, must long prevent it from generally attaining any value at all. . . . The plan which, it appears to me, would be best calculated to secure to the people the fruits of their industry, and to Government a permanent revenue, is comprised under the following heads. . . .

1. A reduction of fifteen per cent. to be made on the lease assessment.

2. The country to be rented immediately of Government by small farmers, as at present, every one receiving just as much land as he demands.

3. Settlements to be annual; that is to say, every man to be permitted to give up, or take, whatever land he pleases every year.

4. Every man to have a part, or the whole, of his lands in lease, who wishes it; and in order to encourage the application for leases, all lands held under annual tenures, to be taken from the occupants and given to such other farmers as may demand them in lease, on their paying to Government, as purchase-money, one year's rent for any particular field, or one half-year's rent for the whole farm.

5. Villages and districts to be responsible for all individual failures.

The following regulations are from my letter of the 18th July last—

6. All lands included in the lease, should remain invariably at the rent then fixed, after the proposed reduction of fifteen per cent.

7. All lands not included in the lease, should be rented at the average of the village to which they belong.

8. Lands included in the lease, being given up and allowed to be waste for any number of years, should, when again occupied, pay, the very first year, the full rent as before.

9. All castes, whether natives or aliens, to pay the same rent for the same land.

10. No additional rent ever to be demanded for improvements. The farmer who, by digging a well, or building a tank, converts dry land into garden or rice-fields, to pay no more than the original rent of the ground.

11. No reduction of the established rent ever to be allowed, except where the cochineal-plant, mulberry, etc., are cultivated.[1]

Munro thus admitted that all the advantages of the lease system could be secured by the ryotwari settlement proposed by Read, indeed that the former was definitely unsuitable for Salem owing to both 'the poverty, the ignorance, and the manners of the people' and the 'ignorance and inexperience of the British'.[2] He did not preclude the possibility that as conditions improved leases might be introduced which would enable government to 'ascertain accurately the probable amount of collections',[3] but, he wrote to his father in the next year,

I rather wish to continue the plan now followed, which consists in letting every farmer please himself; he may take as much or as little land as he pleases every year; he may reject his old fields and take new; he may keep a part of the whole for one year or twenty, as he finds it most convenient; and as every field has a rate of assessment, which never varies, he knows perfectly what he has to trust to, and that his rent can never rise or fall but exactly in proportion to the extent of the land he occupies.[1]

Munro and Read had reached agreement on the form of revenue settlement best suited to the Baramahal, but they had not carried the Board of Revenue with them. Read appears to have ignored the Board in making his settlements, and failed to reply to their requests for information. As a soldier and man of action he seems to have felt some of the scorn for presidency civilians and their theories which Munro was to have trouble in concealing. The Board asked in June 1797 for his opinion, and that of his assistants, on 'the permanent settlement of the districts',[2] and repeated the enquiry a year later.[3] By this time Read was not only a firm advocate of a ryotwari settlement, but had put it into practice. Taking advantage of his proclamation many of the ryots had cancelled their engagements in lease and thrown up lands they were unable to cultivate, with the result that the jama, or total demand for revenue, in 1797–8 was 54,000 pagodas less than in 1796–7.[4] The reasons for this failure to tell the Board what was being done are not clear. Munro wrote to his father in 1798:

Government have desired . . . [the settlement] to be made so as to sit light upon the inhabitants; but they were not aware that, in order to effect this, they must relinquish twenty or twenty-five per cent of the present revenue. This reduction will be recommended to them by every argument that can be thought of, but I am not sure that they will have resolution enough to agree to it.[5]

If this was the plan it was not carried out: one suspects that Read wished to wait till the revenue had made that marked improvement which he believed would follow eventually after the change to a ryotwari settlement, before giving the Board a chance to consider his work. In this he was shrewd; no written advocacy, least of all

Read's somewhat tortuous arguments, was likely to carry much weight with a Board presented with a large loss of revenue. Before the expected improvement had taken place, however, the Board recorded that they had 'understood that the Jummah fixed for 1204 [1794-5] was to be considered in force until a survey of the lands was made, and a quinquennial lease ... completed progressively as the Survey of each district was finished'. They now learnt for the first time that this had not been carried out, and that the lease system 'had been relinquished for another plan of annual settlement', an action for which authority was 'vested in Government alone' and which the Board therefore disapproved. They called for a prompt and minute explanation for the change which resulted in such a loss of revenue.[1] In May 1799, before Read had given the explanation demanded, war with Tipu began once more, and he and Munro were recalled to their military duties. By this time Read possibly had become a little sceptical about the advantages of the ryotwari settlement,[2] though if he had doubts he kept them from the Board. He had presented the Board with an exhaustive report on the state of the district, but his promised explanation of the 'effects of annual and lease Settlements on the Inhabitants' and his 'plan for the final settlement of the Ceded Districts' were never written, a failure which the Board did not ascribe to 'neglect, want of zeal for the public service or of ability', but which they much regretted had been caused by 'avocations foreign to his Revenue duties'.[3]

The main concern of Read and Munro in the Baramahal, once order had been established, had been with evolving an efficient method of collecting the land revenue. It was in this, too, that Munro profited most from working under Read. The judicial side of their administration was rudimentary, the government at this time believing a permanent settlement of the revenue to be necessary before a system of courts, judges and judicial regulations could be introduced. Read does not appear to have thought much about the problem, and on the two great questions raised by

Cornwallis's reforms in Bengal—the extent to which the Company's servants should assume the everyday administration of justice, and the degree to which judicial power should be separated from that of the executive—he gave no clear answers. His general view seems to have been 'that any man of moderate ability and equitable notions of right and wrong cannot frequently err in his judgment'.[1] Munro, however, had definite answers to both questions; he had come to his own conclusions, and these were far from coinciding with the Bengal system. He did not share Read's confidence in the simple application of 'equitable notions of right and wrong', believing that the imperfect knowledge of the language and customs of the people possessed by the British made it difficult, especially in cases concerning property, to reach a correct judgment.

I have found myself so often mistaken [he wrote] in cases which I thought I had investigated with the greatest caution previous to passing sentence that I now generally confine myself to criminal matters and leave all those of property to panchayet. What presumption in us to determine three or four causes in a night each of which would take up a panchayet several days.[2]

Not only was it presumption to attempt to settle large causes in an inadequate time, but there was the danger that once started on civil cases, the collectors' time would be fully taken up with 'petty disputes in villages about Washermen and Barbers'.[3] Practical considerations led Munro to the view that 'it is among themselves that nations must in most cases look for justice', but at this time his view of the result of such a policy was a pessimistic one:

when the manners of a whole people are so depraved as to render them liable on every occasion to be influenced by motives of fear or corruption it is in vain to expect that substantial justice can be generally administered. I am afraid that there is no means by which this object can ever be attained until the principles of morality shall become more respected among the natives than they are at present.[4]

Munro doubted whether the separation of the judicial from the executive power, one of the foundations of the Cornwallis system in Bengal, would produce any good.[1] The argument that the union of judicial and executive power would destroy the liberty of the people was irrelevant, he believed, where the people were already 'under a foreign dominion, and can look for nothing more than the preservation of their own laws and customs, so far as they are compatible with the security of the authority of that Government'.[2] The nature of judicial office would prevent its holder from acquiring the same knowledge of the people as was possessed by a revenue officer, and therefore render him more liable to be deceived in his judgments. Added to this was the fact that a large proportion of litigation was about 'the boundaries of fields, stray cattle, the wages of farmers' servants, or the shares of their partners; and as they are connected with revenue', wrote Munro, 'they could no way be so easily or so expeditiously settled as by the collector and his tahsildars, or by punchayats under their direction.'[3] Munro would allow 'a superior court' to which appeals could be made from the decisions of the collector, but this should not interfere with the interior management of his district in which he should possess the whole authority, civil and judicial. To establish separate courts of justice in the district, Munro concluded, would greatly increase the expense of government and impede the collection of the revenue, 'without the smallest benefit to the people'.[4]

Read's settlement of the Baramahal was later criticised for producing 'a most unequal, and in general an over-assessment of the country',[5] and it is clear that on the whole this judgment was justified. Read grasped certain principles, such as that the assessment should be fixed on each field, after its extent had been measured and its soil classified. He failed however, both logically, when he modified the assessment according to the health, strength, stock and other circumstances of the cultivator; and in practice, when none of his assistants except Munro gave the assessment the care essential for its success. These shortcomings must not detract from the importance of his achievement. For all its imperfections

33

his ryotwari system had in itself the seed of improvement. By bringing the government servants into close touch with the affairs of every village, the way was made clear for the reform of abuses and the improvement of the system. This Munro was to go on to do.

CHAPTER 2

THE SETTLEMENT OF KANARA

1799–1800

In 1797, a damaged French frigate put in at Mangalore and the unscrupulous adventurer Ripaud presented himself to Tipu as an envoy from Mauritius, and asked for help against the British. Since the Treaty of Seringapatam in 1792 the British had looked upon Tipu's behaviour as evincing 'the most hostile sentiments' towards their government, and as showing 'that he only waited for an opportunity of attacking its power',[1] and their view seemed confirmed when Ripaud and two Mysorean envoys were sent off to Mauritius bearing an intemperate proclamation lauding the French republican constitution, proclaiming Tipu's undying hatred of the English, and announcing that he was only waiting for French help 'to declare war against the English, whom he ardently desires to expel from India'.[2] The Governor of Mauritius, with an extraordinary blindness for the consequences, made this message public: Wellesley was only too ready to take it at its face value, and on the landing at Mangalore in April 1789 of about one hundred Frenchmen and half-castes from the French frigate *La Preneuse*, he took the view 'that an immediate attack upon Tippoo Sultaun, for the purpose of frustrating the execution of his unprovoked and unwarrantable projects of ambition and revenge, appeared to be demanded by the soundest maxims of justice and policy'.[3] Delay was enforced by the complete lack of readiness at Madras, and by the general opinion against precipitate action. This was not shared by Munro.

Our Government [he wrote to his father] are anxious to avoid a war: they are alarmed at the expense, and dread the event. For my own part, I think the sooner we have it, the better, and that it is the only thing that can make amends for the

35

extreme folly of the last peace. We never can be safe, while such a power as Tippoo exists; nor can the Carnatic be secure, till we have Seringapatam.[1]

Wellesley used the time to try to revive the former alliance with the Nizam and the Peshwa and to prepare for action. At the end of 1798 he began a correspondence with Tipu, who, apparently well aware of the odds against him, sent prevaricating and evasive replies. These, Wellesley chose to regard as a 'deliberate insult', and in February 1799 he wrote exultantly to Lord Grenville: 'I have had the satisfaction to succeed completely in drawing the Beast of the jungle [Tipu] into the toils ... our own army is the finest which ever took the field in India; and by dint of scolding and flattering I have equipped it within a period of time perfectly astonishing to the old school.'[2]

The British campaign was brilliantly successful. Two armies closed on Seringapatam from the east and west. Tipu struck one blow at each and lost over 2,000 men, after which he withdrew to his capital. From there he tried to negotiate, but the British terms enraged him with 'the arrogance and tyranny of the conditions. .... it was better to die like a soldier', he bitterly concluded, 'than to live a miserable dependent on the infidels'.[3] Seringapatam was stormed on 4 May, and Tipu died, fighting as a soldier, with 8,000 of his men. The British losses exceeded 1,100. Following the victory came the settlement. Wellesley decided to keep a central Kingdom of Mysore and to place on the throne a representative of the former dynasty. The bulk of the territory left was to be divided between the Company and the Nizam with a small area in the north-west going to the Peshwa, on certain conditions, in spite of the fact that Wellesley considered his conduct to have been 'such as to forfeit every claim upon the faith and justice of the Company'.[4] As Wellesley probably expected, the conditions were not accepted and that territory too was divided between the Nizam and the Company. The British acquired the town and island of Seringapatam, Wynad in the south-west, the districts of Coimbatore and Dharapuram in the south, and in the west,

Kanara, a narrow strip along the coast about 230 miles in length and 40 in breadth at its widest part. Munro was critical of the settlement. Rather than produce a child of seven to become raja of Mysore, he would have divided the country equally with the Nizam. 'We have now made great strides in the South of India', he wrote. 'Many think we have gone too far; but I am convinced that the course of events will still drive us on, and that we cannot stop until we get to the Kistna.'[1]

A commission to settle the Mysore government and to make the partition treaty was set up at the end of May; Munro and Captain John Malcolm were appointed joint secretaries, and in July it was decided to place Munro in charge of the civil administration of Kanara,[2] with Alexander Read,[3] a nephew of his chief in the Baramahal, as assistant collector. Munro hesitated to accept the appointment. He was reluctant to leave the Baramahal just when the great labour of settlement was finished and when he 'anticipated the pleasure of sitting down ... and enjoying a few years of rest after so many of drudgery'.[4] After a severe attack of fever early in 1799 he was doubtful whether his health would stand continuance of the privations of a life in tents investigating the revenues of a new country. The revenue of Kanara, he believed, had been over-estimated, and to attempt to bring it to its estimated value in a short time could only lead to a 'certain unavoidable loss of reputation'.

But [Munro wrote to the Governor-General] I considered it was my duty to go, and the more especially as I was conscious that though I should never be able to realize any sanguine ideas that might be entertained on the subject of the revenue of Canara I should yet, from possessing the advantages of long experience, be enabled to render it as productive as it could have been in any other hands.[5]

He also had the idea that the financial advantages of accepting the position might enable him to return 'a year or two sooner to Europe' than he could have done by remaining in the Baramahal.[6]

Munro's first task in Kanara was to establish order.

When I entered Canara from the southward in July last [he wrote later], the districts of Coomlah and Vittel, lying between Bekul and Mangalore were in the possession of two chiefs styling themselves Rajahs, who had long been pensioners of the Bombay government. Jummalabad had refused to surrender. A great part of the country, from Neliserum to Barkoor, had been ravaged by the Coorugs. In many places the cattle had been swept away, the villages burnt, and the inhabitants—men, women, and children—carried off into captivity. The followers of Dhondajee had made an irruption from Beddanore into the district of Cundapore; Bilghee was in the possession of a poligar; Ankolah and Sadasewagur were garrisoned by the Sultan's troops, and the Rajah of Sondah had entered that district as his ancient inheritance.[1]

Munro's treatment of the Kumla poligar (military chieftain) was typical of his methods of dealing with that class. Before the invasion of the country by Haidar this man's ancestors were styled rajas, and were hereditary managers of their several districts. Their assessment, however, according to Munro, 'was regarded not as a peshcush but as rent, for it was nearly as high as that which was paid by Potails or ordinary renters for Districts of equal value'.[2] In 1784 the raja, in exile in Tellicherry, was placed by the British on a pension of 200 rupees monthly, but on the English invasion of Tipu's territory, the family looked for reinstatement in their old position. The poligars of Bilgi, Sunda and Vithal did likewise, and Munro found similar pretenders to almost every district of Kanara.

During the war these poligars had been issued with arms from the Company's store, and the raja of Kumla had entered the district he claimed with a party of banditti and had levied contributions. Munro first sent proclamations to all the occupied districts warning the inhabitants not to pay any balances except to persons under his authority. The poligars were told they must personally lay their claims before the Resident of Mysore, and that these could only be heard when they had withdrawn all their followers from the Company's territory. Not one of them obeyed. The rajas of Kumla and Vithal, before Munro's arrival in the district, had been ordered by General Hartley, commanding the military force, to return to Malabar and deliver up the arms they had received. The Kumla poligar complied personally, but left a nephew behind with a body of armed followers who, for two months, successfully prevented any of the inhabitants from making a settlement with Munro. Munro took no notice of the nephew or the force. They were, he wrote, 'too strong for the civil power, but at the same time too contemptible to be made the object of a military expedition, when the troops were required for more important services'. He was also 'averse to us using force wherever a point could be accomplished by patience and fair means'.[1] In time, General Hartley having threatened to treat the nephew as a rebel, and the Commissioners of Malabar having stopped the poligar's pension until the arms were returned, they were given up and the nephew desisted from opposing the authority of the amildar sent by Munro. The poligar's conduct was, Munro considered, 'extremely irregular'. But, he added, 'this must always be expected when we avail ourselves of the assistance of such allies'.[2] At the commencement of Cornwallis's war against Tipu the poligar had received assurances of being reinstated in his ancient district should it be taken from Tipu, and in 1799 the Commissioners of Malabar led him to believe that in the event of victory against Tipu he would be entitled to something more than his usual pension. For these reasons Munro recommended[3] doubling his pension on condition that neither he, nor any of his family, should ever live in Kumla, and this the government agreed to do.[4]

The Vithal poligar, who had been pensioned by the Bombay government, in the same way as the Kumla poligar, caused more trouble. He ignored the summons from the Commissioners of Malabar to give up the Company's arms and returned to Vithal with a number of followers. He took over the management of the district and collected the revenue, maintaining his position, according to Munro, entirely by terror. Early in 1800 he combined with other disaffected elements in south Kanara—a body of peons led by Suba Rao, formerly a sarishtadar in Tipu's service and now following Kisnam Kayak, and a party of Moplas, of Arab descent, to whom belonged 'most of the Thieves and robbery and murders of Malabar'.[1] Vithal Hagada, as the poligar was called, also set up a Muslim with the title of Fatha Haidar, and emissaries were sent to all the patels exhorting them to rise and join the rebels. Munro never doubted that his peons with fifty sepoys could put down the rebellion, as there was no general support in the country for the insurgents. 'After all the alarm of general insurrection', he wrote in a private letter, 'I imagine I will have less trouble with Futteh Hyder than with [the Accountant General]'.[2] Suba Rao was defeated by a party of peons, Fatha Haidar was surprised and routed with the loss of forty or fifty men killed and wounded,[3] and on 18 June 1800 Munro reported that 'the force of banditti is now entirely dispersed every where except in Vittel'.[4] These two having been driven up the Ghats, Munro was enabled to turn his attention to Vithal. Munro had raised over 1,000 military peons,[5] and on 9 July a force of about 850 peons entered Vithal, defeated the rebels, and took the whole of Hagada's family. This force was joined by a party of one hundred sepoys under Captain Bruce, sent at Munro's request, and on 18 July Vithal Hagada gave himself up. It had at one time been Munro's intention that this man too should be treated like the Kumla poligar and be given an increased pension,[6] but on the news of the capture he wrote to Colonel Close, the Resident in Mysore:

We may now by making an example of him and his associates secure Canara from internal disturbances in the future. . . . It is the mistaken notion of observing on this coast towards every petty chief of a District all the ceremony and attention that is due to a sovereign which keeps alive idle and dangerous pretensions which it ought rather to be our aim to extinguish.[7]

Vithal Hagada was hanged.[8]

In addition to the disturbances within Kanara, there was a threat to its northern districts, for almost all the time that Munro was there, from Dundia Wagh, a Maratha irregular soldier of great energy and capacity who had been forcibly converted and then imprisoned by Tipu but had escaped on the fall of Seringapatam. His aim was the establishment of a new dynasty in south India. He raised a force of followers but in August 1799 suffered a defeat from British forces and fled north into the Maratha country— where, however, he was attacked by Gokhale, a Maratha chief on the frontier. Early in 1800 Dundia was reported to be plotting to get one of Tipu's sons into his hands, and was building up his force and plundering near Kittur and Darwar, just north of the British frontier. His progress was such as to induce Colonel Arthur Wellesley in April to order three regiments of cavalry into the field and northward. At almost the same time the fortress of Jumalabad in South Kanara, which had not been captured by the British until October 1799, fell into the hands of a rebel force of deserters from British forces, and until it was retaken in June troops had to be kept in the south that Wellesley could well have used against Dundia. On 21 April Wellesley wrote rather irascibly:

Surely if the Mahratta Government is anything but a name, it may be made either to crush this man, to allow us to destroy him, or to avow him. He either belongs to the Mahrattas or he does not. . . . Our tranquillity in this country has really depended for these last four months on the contests between Goklah and Dhoondiah. . . . I think that the tranquillity of a great nation ought to have a more firm foundation.[1]

By the beginning of May Dundia had taken possession of Dummul, had been joined by 'Rajahs, Polygars, and disaffected and discontented of all descriptions'[2] including 'almost the whole of Tippoo's cavalry',[3] was moving nearer the British frontier, and, according to unsubstantiated reports, was in touch with poligars in Kanara itself. 'It is very clear', Arthur Wellesley wrote, 'that the name of Dhoondiah is made use of among all the Company's turbulent subjects to create disturbances.'[4] On 25 May Wellesley was ordered to attack Dundia, if necessary pursuing him over the frontier into the Maratha territory. Wellesley followed him with persistence, seeking to force him into the open. On 26 July Dummul was stormed and taken, on 30 July Dundia's camp was attacked. By this time his followers were deserting him. The decisive action was on 10 September, when his army of 5,000 horse was entirely defeated and dispersed, and Dundia himself was killed.[1]

Munro did not have an easy time with the continued military operations in the districts under his charge, and with troops marching through on their way to the neighbouring territories in the north and east. At one time there were fourteen military stations in Kanara, and there was a constant change of commanding officers, with all of whom Munro had to communicate. 'If I had had the command in Canara', he wrote to Thomas Cockburn[2] in June 1800, 'it would have greatly facilitated the settlement, and possibly have prevented some of the disturbances which have since happened; but I hardly see how this can be brought about, with so many seniors to myself serving in every corps.'[3] He was in the invidious position of being expected by the army to ensure a constant supply of grain and cattle for it, to raise peons when necessary, and often to provide money to pay the troops; while the inhabitants under his care sent to him their complaints about forcible purchases and unfair prices. The whole problem was exacerbated by the multiplicity of coins in circulation and the confused rates of exchange.

Munro's view on the provision of grain was quite clear-cut and definite.

Every man ought certainly to be allowed to sell his Grain, or not, as he pleases, and to put his own price upon it, for it is the right of every inhabitant to get as good a price as he can. Should the price rise so high that the Troops cannot purchase it, the Rayet is not on this account to reduce his price. It becomes, then, the business of Government to find Grain for their Troops on the best terms they can.[4]

Cattle were scarce and of poor quality in Kanara, but Munro was equally insistent that the inhabitants must be paid for them at the price usually obtained, and not at some arbitrary price set by the

troops. If such a fair price was paid he saw little need for his interference; but in fact it was not always paid. In June 1800 Munro
wrote to the Board of Revenue reporting that guards had been sent
out to drive in cattle at an arbitrary price. Munro had no authority
to stop them, but requested that he should be authorised to make
up the price of the beasts. Whatever else, 'the Inhabitants ought
... to be paid for their property'. The Board agreed with his
attitude.[1] While Colonel Arthur Wellesley argued that in general
those charged with the civil administration ought not to interfere
with the military purchases, the principle broke down in practice,
and he envisaged cases 'in which such an interference may be not
only proper but absolutely necessary'. When he came to the
conclusion that one of Munro's amildars in Sunda was making it
difficult to procure supplies for the troops, he quietly threatened:
'all I can say upon the subject is, that if the grain is not procured, I
do not conceive that I am answerable for the consequences'.[2]

What emerges most clearly from Munro's correspondence about
supplies, with military officers and the Board of Revenue alike, is
his firm backing for what he believed to be the rights of the ryots
under his care: 'it was the business of Government to take care of
their Army'.[3] The fact that he himself was an army officer (he was
promoted major in May 1800), always hankering to be on the
field of action, and believing that British power must rapidly be
extended in the south of India, was not incompatible with this
regard for Indian welfare; but not many of his military contemporaries shared his view.

In dealing with the intricacies of the currency used in Kanara,
his attitude is again made clear. Writing to Colonel Sartorius, then
commanding officer in the district, Munro asked for orders to be
published that all coins sent to the bazaar should pass at bazaar
exchange and not at that decided by the paymaster. The troops
might in consequence of this measure sustain a very heavy loss—
'but whatever the loss may be it certainly ought to be made good
by Government and not by the Inhabitants'.[4] When the British

entered the country great quantities of 'Porto Novo pagodas', previously unknown there, were taken in to pay the troops. These were overvalued in terms of the current 'Bahaderi pagodas', and both were issued to the troops at too high a nominal value. 'It was supposed that an order from [Munro] would be sufficient to make them current in the country' at the prescribed rates, but this he did not attempt.[1] There was nothing singular about Kanara in this problem; different presidencies had different moneys of account (in Bombay silver, in Madras gold), provincial mints issued coins different in denomination and value from those issued at the Presidency, and almost every 50 miles there was a different current money. In a letter to the Governor-General,[2] Munro, after describing the problem, advocated abolishing all provincial mints and making the current money of Bengal the current money of Madras and Bombay. He saw no objection of any weight to an immediate execution of this plan. Its disadvantages would be negligible, the benefits immense.

There is perhaps no code or regulation [he wrote] that could be framed for the extension of agriculture and commerce and for the advancement of general prosperity that would so surely and speedily attain these ends as the simple measure of establishing an uniform currency to serve both as the current money and the money of account upon the three Establishments.[3]

Until the beginning of February 1800 Munro was under the direction of the Commissioners at Mysore, but he was then put under the Board of Revenue at Fort St George. The Board wrote to him that before furnishing him with instructions, they awaited his report on the state of the districts under his charge, together with as much information as he had acquired and an account of the arrangements made for the collection of the revenue. In general he was to 'keep in view as much as possible' the principles of the permanent settlement.[4] Munro replied that it would be some time before he could provide the details they required,[5] and that he had yet to complete the revenue settlement of Sunda. Besides the confusion caused by the poligars, and the occupation of some districts by hostile forces for several months after his arrival, the violence of the monsoon from July till October caused delay in assembling the inhabitants to settle their rents. This delay was increased by the widely dispersed population, 'for both in Canara and Sondah it is only Bazarmen fishermen etc. who live in Villages. The Cultivators of the soil almost universally dwell in detached habitations, every man upon his own land—so that many days are frequently lost in drawing together from the Jungles the scattered inhabitants of what is called a village.'[1] The final check to rapid progress was the country itself. Kanara, 'rude and savage beyond all description',[2] seven times as long as it is wide, is crossed by a vast number of rivers, running down to the sea from the mountains which stretch the length of its eastern boundary. There was scarcely a road passable except along the sea coast, and where there were no roads Munro found he had to walk, for it was too rugged for riding.[3] On the inland roads bullocks could not travel fully loaded and tents had to be carried by coolies. The army marched along the coast, sending its tents by sea, and occupying the houses of the inhabitants. When it moved inland, as it did to Jumalabad, it moved parallel to the rivers, and thus avoided crossing them. But Munro 'never moved without crossing a river, and often two or three'.[4] He could not use elephants to carry his equipment, as loading and unloading them at the rivers would take all day, and 'even with bullocks', he wrote, 'the business of swimming them over takes up so much time, that I am always obliged to wait an hour or two for my tent'.[5] Ten miles a day was as much as his kachahri could go on an average, and it was impossible to 'go the rounds' of Kanara and Sunda by any road short of 650 miles.[6]

In spite of the incessant interruptions to the task of settling the revenue of Kanara and Sunda, Munro finished it in April 1800, and on 31 May sent to the Board of Revenue a report on its 'ancient and present state'.[7] To write this report, he told Cockburn, he had been forced to go through more labour among sanads and accounts than he had ever undergone before, or believed he would have time to do again in the future.[1] He considered his job was to investigate and report, and leave it to the Board to decide on the expediency of lowering the assessment. But there was no possibility of the Board's failing to understand what he believed, on the facts, to be the wisest course of action, as had been the case with Read's reports on the Baramahal. Throughout his pages Munro hammered home, again and again, the overwhelming importance of a moderate assessment.[2] It was not the first time he had stressed this,[3] but from the history of Kanara he was able to draw copious evidence to support his contention.

Much of Munro's difficulty in completing his first settlement he put down to the particular state of land tenure in Kanara. He thought that before Haidar's conquest all lands were private property, the land rent, or more accurately land tax, being fixed, and 'probably lighter than that of any other province in India';[4] but the amildars of Haidar and Tipu had laid on one assessment after another until the rate of revenue was as high as in Mysore. These impositions had never been peacefully accepted. In 1796 Tipu had been forced to promise a reduction, and the advent of British power, the inhabitants believed, was their chance to have the assessment lowered. Munro found that wherever he went the people sent in a paper, 'a kind of bill of rights, stating this deduction promised by Tipu as the only preliminary on which they could agree to come to any discussion of their settlements' [Para. 3]. Munro refused to accept any previous stipulations, and finding him inflexible the ryots eventually came in to the kachahri. Thus, apart from the difficulties in districts claimed by poligars, such as Kumla and Vithal, the obstacles met in the settlement of Kanara were attributed by Munro entirely to 'the inhabitants having once been in possession of a fixed land-rent, and in their still universally possessing their lands as private property' [Para. 4].

All later assessments of Kanara, Munro believed, had as their basis the assessment made in the middle of the fourteenth century by Harihara I, the raja of Vijayanagar, on the principles laid down in the Sastras, which supposed the produce to be to the seed as twelve to one, and prescribed the proportions in which the produce was to be divided between the sarkar and the cultivator.[1] This settlement was not supposed to have been based on actual measurement, but 'merely on a rough estimate of the seed sown in each field' [Para. 8]. Various additions were made to this assessment under the Vijayanagar and Bijapur governments, and were written down not only in the general accounts of the districts, but in those of every individual landholder. All subsequent additions were regarded as 'oppressive exactions'. Between Kanara and Mysore and its neighbours was the great distinction that the land revenue of the former was fixed upon the land, and did not, as in the latter, fluctuate from year to year according to the supposed ability of the cultivator. And in Kanara, Munro reported, the ancient assessment, whatever in fact its details had been, 'appears to have been sufficiently moderate to have enabled the country to attain a high degree of cultivation and the inhabitants as much comfort and security as could be expected under an arbitrary government.'[2]

Had such an assessment as that introduced by Hyder existed in ancient times [Munro wrote] Canara would have long ago been converted into a desert. In a country so rocky and uneven, where cattle are not only scarce, but, even where they are to be had, cannot always be employed; where every spot, before it can be cultivated, must be levelled with great labour by the hand of man—the expense of the first preparation of waste ground must have been so great, that it could never have been attempted, unless the assessment had been extremely moderate; and even after land has been brought into cultivation; if it is neglected for a few years, it is soon broken up by the deep gullies formed by the torrents which fall during the monsoon [Para. 16].

The results of the rule of Haidar and Tipu were dire enough. The population of Kanara had decreased, and formerly flourishing towns contained only a few inhabitants. Honawar, once the second town in trade after Mangalore, had not a single house, and

Mangalore itself was greatly decayed. Many things contributed to this ruin: there had been four wars since Haidar's invasion, Tipu himself had destroyed many of the coastal towns, inhabitants had been forcibly moved, and there was the general disorder and corruption of Tipu's government. But taken altogether, Munro believed, these did not count so much as the 'extraordinary augmentation of the land rent' [Para. 18]. Haidar, by regarding the province as a fund from which he might draw without limit for the expenses of his military adventures, had ruined Kanara. Tipu's demands were as insatiable, his management much less efficient.

When the Vijayanagar assessment was made, the whole of the land was parcelled out among a 'prodigious number' of small proprietors, holding lands with annual taxes of from 5 to 5,000 pagodas [£2–£2,000].[1] Munro's researches led him to the view that estates were all regarded as private property, were transferable by gift or sale, and the sarkar—i.e. government—had no other right in them than what it derived from its claim to the fixed 'rent'. When an inam was granted for the endowment of a temple, or a jagir to an individual, the sarkar could do no more than grant its right to the rent; the only difference to the landholder was that now, instead of paying his rent to government, he paid it to the Brahman of a temple or to an inamdar. The inamdar had no claim to the management of the land, nor could he live on it; 'he was merely a pensioner, whose pension was assigned upon a particular landlord' [Para. 28]. In reforming the revenue system of Kanara, therefore, there were no new rights the government could give to private property in land. The value of the property could be raised by diminishing the assessment, 'but the right itself is already as strong as purchase or prescription can make it, and is as well understood as it is in Great Britain' [Para. 29].

Having completed his account of the development of the assessment and of the nature of landed property in Kanara, Munro finished the report with a few observations on what the rate of assessment ought to be [Para. 33]. Haidar and Tipu had raised the assessment as high as it could be, not infrequently higher than the land could bear, and they should not be taken as a guide. While their level of taxation might be reached in good years, without some reduction the land would never become generally saleable. The assessment, Munro wrote, ought to be made at no higher rate than under the Bijapur government at the time of Haidar's invasion, and he recommended a reduction to that level. 'Whether', he concluded, 'the Board may think it expedient to adopt the assessment here proposed or any other as the foundation of a permanent settlement, it is very clear that . . . it must be greatly below the existing one' [Para. 37].

Munro rightly suspected the Board would be averse to making the reductions he had proposed before the permanent settlement was made,[1] but he admitted to Cockburn that while 'the sooner the inhabitants experience the benefit of an abatement of rent the better', it could be deferred; for Kanara, while not as prosperous as it should have been, was in as good a condition as the Baramahal. A reduction of the customs on rice which he had recommended [Para. 29], however, he believed should be made at once if the revenue was not to be adversely affected.[2] It is clear, too, that in his report of 31 May Munro recommended reductions great enough to cover every possible contingency, in the belief that he might be suddenly called upon to make a permanent settlement. In the next five months he came to take a more favourable view of the situation of the landlords, and in his report of 19 November 1800[3] admitted that he was satisfied that a smaller amount than he had before advocated would answer every purpose of the reduction in the assessment [Para. 2].

In the four months from May, during which the monsoon kept him at Kandapur, Munro had heard numberless disputes over landed property. 'In the Baramahal', he wrote, 'a dispute about land scarcely came before me once in six months; in this country every other cause of litigation or complaint seems to be lost in that of land' [Para. 3]. Where land was so much the object of contention, Munro believed there to be no danger of the inhabitants being unable to pay their taxes, 'for men would hardly lose their time, and spend their money, for the sake of acquiring that which is not worth the holding, or which might involve them in loss' [Para. 3].

The best guide to the reductions needed in the assessment would be the value attached to land by its occupants, but this was difficult to discover, as long experience had taught them that concealment was their best defence against new exactions. Munro wrote in his journal:

I have often asked boys of eight or ten years old, whom I have seen perched on a little scaffold in a field, throwing stones from a sling to frighten the birds, how many bushels they expected when the corn was cut. The answer was always— 'There is nothing in our house now to eat. The birds will eat all this, and we shall be starved.' [1]

There were two other ways of discovering the value of the land. The first was a survey, and this Munro had begun in one district, but its progress was slow and the expense great: there were no trained surveyors in Kanara and they had to be brought in, and their work was complicated by the broken nature of the ground and its intricate subdivision into small portions.[2] The second way was to keep a register of the rents and produce of all lands that became subject to litigation, and Munro was convinced that by keeping such a register 'for two or three years' it would be possible 'to form a more accurate judgment of the average produce than could be done from a survey'.[3]

Among the cases which had come before him, the landlords' rent was much oftener above than below 50 per cent of the net produce [Para. 6], and while there were great inequalities in the proportion of the net produce taken as revenue, the disparities Munro believed to be 'oftener owing to the different proportions of labour bestowed on the land than to those of the assessment' [Para. 7]. As far as the actual realisation of the revenue was concerned, it was not affected by the general question of the justice or injustice of the assessment. It was paid readily, and any outstanding balance was due, not to failure on the part of the inhabitants, but to the disturbances during the British occupation of the country, which had hindered the revenue servants from carrying on the collections, or remitting what had been collected to the treasury.[1] But Munro was far from satisfied merely to collect the greatest possible revenue. 'If we aim not merely at the obtaining of a certain sum as revenue', he wrote, 'but also at giving a new spirit to agriculture, and raising the country to a pitch of prosperity beyond what it has ever been in former times, the present assessment must be lowered' [Para. 4]. He recommended reductions to bring the assessment down to half the net value of the produce.

From the assessment Munro went on to discuss the size of the estates from which the government should collect the revenue. His preference for a settlement with small landholders, cultivating the soil themselves, had become clear while he was in the Baramahal.[2] But his arguments to support it had then been based on the practical advantages of such a scheme. The private property in land which he found in Kanara introduced another factor, and there, he wrote, 'great proprietors cannot be established without annihilating all the rights of the present landlords'. 'Nor do I believe', he added, 'that by any arrangement for placing a number of small estates under the collection of one head landlord any facility in collection, any security for revenue, would be obtained that may not be obtained from letting the estates as they now stand' [Para. 17]. The argument that only large estates would have the resources to develop cultivation to its greatest extent was based, he suggested, on an estimate of farming costs in England rather than in India; and even if it should be valid, such estates, in the absence of entails, of restraints on the transfer of land, and of right of primogeniture, would in a short time be divided into a number of small ones. There was no difficulty in collecting revenue from small proprietors, and as 'the aggregate produce of the land may be, and probably always is, greater with small proprietors than when the whole belongs to a few principal landholders ... Government have therefore a greater fund as the security for their revenue' [Para. 19].

In whatever way I view the question of great and small proprietors [Munro concluded] I am perfectly satisfied that the preference ought to be given to the small ones and that Government ought to make its settlements immediately with them. Under such a system the gross produce of the country will be greater and the collection of the revenue will be as regular as under that of great landholders [Para. 20].

While Munro was 'decidedly in favour of small proprietors', the government had decided to introduce the Bengal system into the Madras territories, and Munro felt it his duty to point out how such a settlement could be accomplished in Kanara. He suggested dividing the country into estates of from 100 to 5,000 pagodas assessment, and making them over to the principal proprietor of the constituent estate. No price could be demanded for the great estates as they would remain private property on which the superior landlord had no claim; there being no new advantage attached to his tenure except a percentage on the revenue he collected, a proprietary right to ownerless waste lands, and the possible benefit through inferior estates—which, on the failure of heirs, formerly went to the sarkar, but would now revert to him. Even these great estates would break down through inheritance unless there was some law of entail. The progress from large estates to small, from revenue settlements with great landlords to settlements with the actual cultivators of the soil, Munro saw, rightly or wrongly, as a general development in India's history. Kanara had progressed further than any other part of the country, and to introduce large estates would be to revert to a more backward stage of social and economic development.

All systems of Indian revenue must, I imagine [he wrote] end in making a direct settlement with every independent landholder without the intervention of any superior lord, and in making every one of them answerable for his own rent and the whole of the estates comprising a village or district answerable for the failure of any estate therein by a second assessment [Para. 22].

In October 1800 the Governor in Council appointed Munro to take charge of the civil administration of territories just ceded to the Company by the Nizam, and Kanara was divided into two collectorates and placed under Alexander Read, who had been one of Munro's assistants, and John Ravenshaw.[1] Munro wrote to them giving some details of his administration, and general instructions.[2] After referring them to his two reports which contained 'every-thing' he had to say on the subject, he warned them of the danger of allowing the kachahri to be placed under the direction of one man, who could acquire such ascendancy that he could do as he pleased 'and keep the Collector in most profound ignorance of what is going forward'. The collector himself must be 'the only head Man'. As so great a part of the land was private property, held at fixed rents, future settlements of the revenue, he wrote, would require little time or labour, because nothing had to be done except to add to the jama of the preceding year the rents of any waste lands that might have been brought into cultivation. Apart from the poligar of Neliserum, who had yet to be finally persuaded to settle quietly on a pension, the territory was at peace.

The contrast with the situation when Munro had assumed responsibility sixteen months before was profound. Munro, how-ever, had never overcome his first aversion to the country. This was repeatedly expressed in his letters to Cockburn: 'I would be very happy to get away from this on any terms'[3]—'Salary is not so much what I want as removal'.[4] The work was unceasing. The whole of the first year was 'a continual struggle against time, to get forward and bring up arrears. In this one year I have gone through more work than in almost all the seven I was in the Baramahl'.[5] Yet just over six months after leaving Kanara Munro was writing to his old chief, Read:

To a revenue man, it is by far the most interesting country in India, and had it not been for the confinement during the five months' monsoon, I never would have left it. All land is private property. . . . In Canara there is already established to our hands all that the Bengal system, supposing it to succeed according to our wishes, can produce in a couple of centuries—a wide diffusion of property, and a permanent certain revenue, not only from the wealth of the inhabitants, but also farther secured by the saleableness of land.[1]

This brings out clearly the importance of Munro's experience in Kanara. It was of course important in the way that any administrator's first charge is important, regardless of its special characteristics. He had to deal directly first with the Commissioners at Mysore and then with the Board of Revenue, rather than with a principal collector set just above him. In February 1800 he asked Cockburn for 'a few hints about the etiquette of writing' to the Board of Revenue; in May and November he drew up two reports which in their clarity, observation and force of argument, show, not a man feeling his way, snowed under with work, but attacking it with quite remarkable energy and capacity. The reports highly impressed both the Madras government and the Court of Directors in London.[2] These reports are more than enough to make us thoroughly wary of accepting Munro's complaint that 'there is so much to do here, that I have not time to *think*'.[3] For he certainly thought, though he might not have realised it. He thought about the private property in land which he believed to exist in Kanara. He thought about the connection between the level of assessment and effectual rights in land; for it was to a moderate and fixed assessment that he attributed the special characteristics of Kanara. He was impressed with the independent 'yeomen' landowners. Kanara was not only the 'most interesting district', it was the most advanced. In the future, he would not be able to look at any district without measuring it against Kanara.

CHAPTER 3

MUNRO IN THE CEDED DISTRICTS
1800–8

During 1800 Wellesley came to believe that a closer and more binding alliance with the Nizam was necessary, and that it was also necessary for the British to strengthen the Nizam's government in face of the threat posed by the Marathas' inclination to view Hyderabad once more as their plundering ground. It was decided to extend the basis of the treaty of 1798 (which had been directed against Tipu) and to make it generally defensive against all powers; in fact, to take the Nizam under the protection of the British government. In return the Nizam, instead of making monetary contributions, surrendered all the territories acquired from Mysore both in 1792 and 1799: all his share of the spoils of the victorious wars against Tipu of Cornwallis and Wellesley now passed to the Company. The country thus surrendered, known as the Ceded Districts, was in area about 20,000 square miles, or larger than Scotland, and contained a population estimated at nearly 2,000,000. The value put upon its revenue when it was ceded was 1,651,545 star pagodas [£660,618], though Munro was to doubt if the whole revenue would 'exceed two-thirds of the schedule'.[1] Lord Clive considered that the best arrangement for its administration would be to 'vest the whole civil government in one Collector with general powers of superintendence and control, and to appoint a sufficient number of inferior Collectors for the execution of the detailed duties of Revenue and Investigation',[2] and Munro was appointed Principal Collector, with James Cochrane, John Ravenshaw, Alexander Stodart and William Thackeray as subordinate collectors.[3] Colonel Arthur Wellesley was ordered to establish British authority with his troops, and in

January 1801 Munro reported that the country was completely occupied.[1]

There was no suggestion by government that Munro should have any more than the normal powers of a collector, and this was a situation with which he was by no means satisfied. To the civil powers he possessed Munro would have added the military. 'Now the best plan after all for organising these Countries', he wrote to Webbe,[2] 'would be to contrive some means of giving me the military command. Weed out the useless dogs above. . . . I am certainly a better General now than I shall be twenty years hence. . . .'[3] The number of subordinate collectors he thought excessive: three would have been much more convenient than four, he wrote, when the government decided to keep Ravenshaw in Kanara but sent Groeme in his place, because they could have been given Divisions without breaking in much upon the boundaries of Districts.[4] Indeed the settlement of the country, in Munro's view, would have been 'most facilitated' if it had been wholly left to him the first year and if two subordinate collectors were appointed in the second year.[5] He preferred to use native amildars rather than inexperienced European assistants, who too often were ignorant of the local language.[6] It soon became clear, however, that Munro's confidence in Indian assistants was not shared by the Board of Revenue.

The principal Indian revenue assistants in Madras were the sarishtadars and amildars or tahsildars. Among the division servants the sarishtadars occupied the first rank, it being their business to keep the whole of the accounts, to make the annual settlements, to watch over the conduct of all revenue servants, and to superintend generally everything connected with the civil administration of the country. In the district the sarishtadar, while having the entire management of the district accounts, acted under the tahsildar, who was in fact a native collector, assisting the division kachahri in making the annual settlement; and where the collector had time to make it with the heads of villages only, the tahsildar made it in detail with the ryots. The importance Munro attached to the work of the division sarishtadars led him to recommend an increase in their allowances, from 100 to 120 pagodas per month [£48].

It is by them [he wrote to the Board of Revenue] that the whole business of Revenue is managed, for I do little more than watch their behaviour. While they preserve their integrity the inferior servants are compelled to follow their example. . . . Were the pay of Sheristadars doubled it would be nothing compared to the advantage of securing their fidelity. When their allowances are inadequate to their station it cannot be hoped that they will have the resolution to maintain their honesty. Corruption then extends through every gradation to the lowest village servant . . . this must always happen where men possessing little principle are placed in situations where they have ample means of robbing the public revenue without enjoying any such salary as might encourage them to resist the temptation.[1]

For similar reasons Munro recommended increases in the allowances of the other division and district revenue servants.

Arguments such as Munro's had been used by Cornwallis in increasing the remuneration of the Company's European servants, and it had been accepted that only by paying such men an adequate salary could a stop be put to the widespread corruption by which they increased their incomes. That similar treatment might encourage the same sort of result among the Indian servants was suggested by Munro (and it was not to be the last time on which he advocated such a step), but was not accepted by the Board of Revenue. The Board wrote that they had attended to Munro's general arguments

with regard to the employment of . . . native servants and in favour of an encreased pay to them but they cannot acquiese in the Expending or . . . [agree that] Fidelity in the ordinary Duties of native revenue Servants may be induced by adequate pay, but [it] can be effectually secured only by an active personal Control on the part of the Collector himself.[2]

It can never be allowed [they wrote] that the administration of the most material points of Revenue management shall be left to native servants who are so far

57

from being governed by any principle of honor, have seldom been found to discharge the trust reposed in them, but under the operation of that Fear which is excited by a vigilant and rigid Controul.[1]

Munro was greatly concerned that the Board chose to interpret his praise for his native assistants' work as implying that he himself was not fully occupied. 'I assert with confidence', he wrote, 'that in no instance has the personal labour of any Collector ever been more unremittingly applied—and that on my part it shall never be relaxed.'[2] The differences between Munro and the Board over his estimates were eventually reconciled,[3] much to the relief of the Governor in Council, who wrote that the 'peculiar difficulties' of Munro's situation rendered 'indispensably necessary that the most liberal confidence should be reposed in' him,[4] but there was no real reconciliation in their differing attitudes to Indian revenue servants.

Munro's first impression of the Ceded Districts was gloomy: 'there is nothing but desolation wherever I have been yet', he wrote. 'A great proportion of the inhabitants of the Ceded Countries was swept away by the famine of 92, and subsequent bad management has prevented them from recovering.'[5] The population was thinly spread, there were few large towns, and the merchants who lived in them were seldom rich and carried on but little trade. All the ryots were armed and lived together in fortified villages, with the result that the cultivation of the country was very unequal, the lands close to the villages being well cultivated, those at a little distance yielding hardly any produce, and all beyond them lying waste. From the decline of the Vijayanagar government until the cession of the districts to the Company, they had experienced unceasing disturbances, war and depredation. Containing the city of Vijayanagar, the capital of the great empire, they became the scene of perpetual struggles between the Mughul government, the Marathas, the raja of Anagundi, Mysore and a number of petty chiefs. Among all those causes which had contributed to the decline in the prosperity and revenue of the districts, none, in

Munro's opinion, had had a greater influence than the first Mysore war, 'for the Ceded districts were then during two campaigns over run by numerous armies of plundering horse, and by hordes of Brinjarries no less destructive—both were alike active in carrying off whatever was valuable and in destroying what they could not remove'.[1] This constant state of warfare had inured the inhabitants to the use of arms, had rendered them impatient of control, led to the fortifying of their villages, and encouraged feuds between almost all neighbouring villages, in which many were taken and burned. It had filled the country with banditti who daily robbed and murdered all travellers who did not submit to their exactions, and had produced 'such a universal spirit of savage independence and opposition to all regular Government that it was every year necessary to besiege a number of villages before their rents could be collected'.[2]

When Munro entered the districts he found that in addition to the Nizam's troops which, not having been paid, were in a state of mutiny and took three months to get out of the country, there were over 30,000 armed peons harassing the inhabitants, led by about eighty poligars and adventurers. These poligars, Munro reported to the Board of Revenue, had achieved their position in a number of ways. Some had originally been renters of districts, or servants of government who had received their villages at first in inam, as a personal allowance for the support of their rank, and had revolted in times of disturbance. Some received their districts at the usual rent, partly as a personal jagir, and partly for the service of a body of horse and foot soldiers. Some were commanders of a body of peons paid in money, not by jagir, then became renters of districts after being absolved from military service, and finally by holding those districts for a number of years during times of confusion, came at last to be denominated zamindars, and to have the term of peshkash substituted for that of rent. In some parts of the country, indeed, almost every head of a village favoured by the natural strength of the country became a poligar, and was regularly installed with all the forms of a prince of an extensive territory.[1]

When Haidar conquered the Ceded Districts he both expelled the poligars, substituting rent for the peshkash, and resumed all inams. But during the first Mysore war the British deemed it expedient to permit all the poligars to return and occupy their ancient possessions. Each fortified himself in his own district, and at the conclusion of the peace they had become so strong that they in some measure assumed independence. From indolence or weakness the Nizam's officers sometimes even invested them with the management of sarkar villages in addition to their own. The Mysore system, in Munro's view, which resumed all poligarships, expelled their turbulent chiefs, and levied an additional body of troops to prevent their return, was in every respect, both for maintaining the authority of government and the tranquillity of the country, infinitely preferable to that of the Nizam—which at greater expense, incurred by the necessity of frequent expeditions, suffered the poligars to retain their power both to commit every kind of depredation, and on every favourable conjuncture to set government itself at defiance.[2] The general corruptness of the Nizam's civil administration and the weakness of his military force encouraged insurrections everywhere, no revenue was collected without a siege, and no sooner was one poligar reduced than another broke out in rebellion.[3]

The instructions which the Madras government gave Munro for dealing with the poligars were brief but by no means clear.[4] While it was indicated that the Governor in Council would go into the claims of the various poligars when he eventually received a report on the actual state of the district, the general principle was at the same time laid down that 'such of the pretensions of the numerous Zemindars and Polygars as may appear to have been revived since the subversion of the Government of Tippoo Sultan' were to be rejected. In the application of this principle Munro was to use his 'prudence and discretion, for', the instructions continued, at the same time that its justice cannot be disputed it may be expedient from considerations of a local nature, particularly with respect to the force appropriable to the Ceded Country, that you should relax from a strict interpretation of these instructions; and that the final determination of the Governor in Council should be reserved either until you may have thoroughly investigated the actual state of the Ceded Country, or until His Lordship may be enabled to apply a more adequate force to the Government of those provinces.

The local circumstances, that is, might alter the way in which the policy was put into effect, rather than in any way altering its end. This seems to be confirmed by the final instruction to Munro, that in view of the

principle on which it is the intention of the Governor in Council to establish proprietory rights in land, it will be expedient that in the course of [Munro's] enquiries [he] should appreciate the advantage to be expected from the continuance of hereditary possessions to the descendents of the antient families—This however [he was told] is a question *exclusively of policy and not of right.*

If the question of keeping the poligars as proprietors of landed estates was in no way to be settled by an investigation of their existing rights, but rather simply as a matter of policy, it is not clear why the governor should look forward to examining their claims at a later date except to determine which of them had possessed recognised rights before 1792. And if this had to be left to the governor's decision, rather than to Munro's, it would obviously be extraordinarily difficult for Munro to carry out his instructions to reject the pretensions of those poligars which had been revived since that date.

The first problem facing Munro was that 'immediate and vigorous assertion of the Company's authority' called for by Lord Clive.[1] 'We had best I think go quietly to work', he wrote to Webbe, 'establish ourselves firmly in the Country and Conciliate the Inhabitants a little before we begin with [the poligars].'[2] So his first efforts were to gain the confidence of the people, and notwithstanding the state of the country, he traversed the whole of it without a single guard of sepoys. Munro's view on the best policy towards the poligars was made quite clear in a characteristic letter to Webbe.

As the whole gang of them was expelled by Hyder and Tippoo tho' restored by the Nizamites I am for turning every soul of them adrift again—or at least for depriving them of all authority either by confining them to a single village each— or by giving them pensions to pray for our Doulit—But tho' this is what I would do if there were no one to call me to account for oppressing fallen royalty—I see many obstacles in the way at present. The Country is too unsettled, and our force consisting chiefly of Cavalry is little calculated for such warfare. . . . An immediate disclosure of our intentions would most likely raise the Polligars in a mass—whereas by delaying our projects till the end of the Fusly our influence will be established —and some of them will by their behaviour give us a pretext for attacking them not as Polligars but as rebels.[1]

At first Munro allowed all the poligars to remain as they were, but raised their revenue assessment so high as to render it impossible for them to maintain any troops except by withholding their revenue payments. This in fact was to change the peshkash, or customary tribute paid by the poligars to government, into a land rent assessed at nearly the same rate as that on the sarkar land. Thus the most dangerous poligars with the greatest number of followers would either have to submit or else provide Munro with an excuse for acting against them.[2] As he expected, the experience of a few months showed that little was to be got from them except by compulsion, as most of them refused to come in to the kachahri to settle their revenue. In March 1801 Munro asked that General Campbell, the military officer commanding in the Ceded Districts, should be 'empowered to try by military process all persons who oppose the Company's Government'.[3] This power the government granted,[4] and Campbell and Munro issued a proclamation to that effect to the inhabitants. After nearly six months in the Ceded Districts, with the revenue year nearly over, and having obtained from the inhabitants 'the strongest assurance of their aversion to poligar authority', Munro at last called out the troops to act against them.[5]

In proceeding against the different chiefs who were in arms and withheld their revenue, Munro took his first measures against those who had no title to the possessions they had seized. Among these the principal was the Vimla poligar. An earlier poligar had been expelled by Haidar in 1766, and from then until 1791 the district was managed by the sarkar officers. That poligar having died, a distant cousin, during the first Mysore war, seized the district, was driven out by the Nizam's troops, but in 1794 managed to establish himself again and to hold on until 1799 when he died. On his death the head peon and other servants, Munro reported, in order to retain the district in their hands set up an old blind man as poligar, claiming that he was a relative of the late chief, and kept him closely as a prisoner. This unwilling pretender was repeatedly summoned by Munro to come into his kachahri but, not surprisingly, did not appear, and eventually General Campbell, on Munro's requisition, sent a force to attack the fort and seize the poligar.[1] The operation was successful, the gates of the fort were blown open, 'the people found in arms were made examples of', and the poligar was taken into custody[2] and given a pension.

This action had various consequences. Its success, and that of others similar, made an impression that was not confined to those particular districts from which the poligars were expelled, but extended to every part of the Ceded Districts, and led to many poligars submitting to the civil authority and accepting the position of common headmen of villages, or receiving government pensions. By the beginning of 1802 Munro was able to report that all the more powerful poligars of the Ceded Districts had been dispossessed, and though temporary disturbances were to be expected for a few years from the great number of petty chiefs who still remained, they would be rather the incursions of banditti, than the insurrections of a force which could make any formidable opposition to government.[3] This proved to be true.

The seizure of the Vimla poligar led also to a protracted correspondence involving Munro, the Madras government and the

Court of Directors, in which Munro, in seeking to justify his policy, made clear his attitude both to the poligars and to the home government. He explained his policy towards the poligars unequivocally, indeed, from the moment he arrived in the Ceded Districts, whether in his official letters to government or in private ones to Webbe (who was after all secretary to government, and on whom Clive leant heavily in making decisions).[1] To Webbe, for example, he wrote,

The object [of completely reducing the poligars] would perhaps be easier accomplished by raising the rent so high as to disable them from keeping armed followers, by seizing territory on every failure as a compensation—by binding them not to levy any extra assessments on the inhabitants, and by making a violation of this engagement a motive for the total resumption of their districts— By following this plan I imagine that there is no doubt but the whole of them would furnish us with good arguments for expelling them—or reducing them to the level of peaceable citizens in the short space of three or four years.[2]

The operation against the Vimla poligar was approved by the Governor in Council,[3] who also later approved Munro's general policy toward the poligars;[4] approved also by the Board of Revenue, who concluded that as the poligar had been 'acting in open rebellion against the Company's authority' the punishment due to that offence had been inflicted 'in the most public and exemplary manner'.[5] Later the Board developed doubts, and in forwarding to the Governor in Council Munro's report on the poligars, dated 20 March 1802, they wrote,

we cannot but wish that the alternative of a moderate assessment on becoming subject to a Government whose principles are so opposite to the vigorous despotism of preceding rulers had offered to the Polligars a motive to subordination and dutiful demeanour rather than by the highest demand ever made on them have rendered punctuality in their payments difficult, thus inducing a failure to be followed by punishment.[6]

Such doubts were not expressed in any of the Board's letters to Munro, much less did they suggest any alternative policy.[7]

The Court of Directors disapproved of the action.[8] Finding themselves unable even to admit the policy of dispossessing the poligars to be 'clear and indisputable', the Court desired that 'every endeavour' should be made to ensure the future fidelity of the poligars 'by the moderation and justice of our demands, and by a course of Government combining conciliation with firmness. ... our wish', they wrote, 'is to uphold and preserve the Poligars in their rights and enjoyments in the soil, whilst we gradually aim at the reduction of their military power.' In a subsequent despatch similar views were expressed:

It is our most positive injunction, that force be never resorted to against any of the Poligars ... unless in case of actual Rebellion, until every lenient and conciliatory measure has been tried without proper effect. ... It is our anxious wish to owe the obedience of the Poligars and of all others of our Tributaries to their confidence in our justice rather than to their dread of our power.[1]

The reasons given them for the proceedings taken against the Vimla poligar did not in their opinion go beyond the principle they understood to be Munro's: 'that no opportunity should be lost of expelling the Poligars'. If this was in fact the case, and if indeed the full extent of the poligar's misconduct had already been stated, the Court must, they wrote, 'entirely disapprove of the conduct of our Government in giving a public and unequivocal sanction to so questionable a measure'. They directed also that Munro should be removed from his position as Collector, and that 'he be not employed in any Revenue Post in future which the violent and mistaken principles of his conduct seem to render him unqualified to fill'.[2]

Munro was far from accepting the Court's criticism. 'I cannot but feel', he wrote to Bentinck, 'that I have been unworthily treated in being called upon like a criminal to vindicate my conduct in having taken in the midst of difficulties the only way of restoring order to the Country.'[3] He failed see to why the Directors should have objected to the expulsion of the Vimla poligar rather than any other.

Men like them [he wrote] at so great a distance could not see so much as those upon the spot the strong necessity which existed at that time for clearing the Country. . . . Lord Clive wished not only to prevent the reestablishment of Polligars in our new acquisitions but to weaken the influence of those in the Carnatic by raising their tribute and disarming them. . . . Though for the sake of privacy and expedition publick discussions were avoided I received many private communications with Lord Clives knowledge approving the expeditions that had taken place and authorizing others to go on. . . . and as I had no doubt of the support and confidence of His Lordships Government I never thought it necessary on any occasion to save myself by waiting for a written order.[1]

In the letter explaining his actions which Munro sent to the Board of Revenue to be forwarded to the Court of Directors[2] he argued that in view of the state of the Ceded Districts in 1801, the reduction of the Vimla poligar had been essential for carrying into effect the government's instructions to establish their authority over the country. His actions, he wrote, had been based on their orders of 25 December 1800, from which he had conceived

that it was the intention of Government that the Ceded Districts with respect to all claims and incumbrances should revert as nearly as possible to the precise state in which they were when ceded by Tippoo Sultan—that as none of the Polligars were in possession of their Pollams during his reign—and that as the Nizam never acknowledged the rights of those who afterwards seized by force a part or the whole of the Districts but on the contrary employed his Troops at all times in operations for their expulsion that consequently I was to reject their claims and dispossess them.[3]

This explanation did not induce the Court to alter their opinion, though they no longer insisted on Munro's removal.[4] Even if they were to accept that the expulsion of the poligars had been, as Munro argued, not the subversion of established rights, but rather the prevention of their re-establishment—that to have admitted the claims of the Vimla poligar (or rather of those who used him to further their own power), who had possessed himself of the whole district, would have encouraged the pretensions of those who had only been able to occupy a single fort or village—the Court, they insisted, could still see no justification for treating the poligar as a rebel, when the extent of his delinquency was nothing more than 'a defective title to the Pollam, and a refusal to obey the Collector's summons to attend his Cutchery'.[1]

The Directors' motives were admirable, though if we accept Munro's claim of the support and approval of Lord Clive,[2] the Court's attitude to Munro would appear to be based on inadequate information, for which Munro could hardly be blamed. Certainly Bentinck shared Munro's views in being satisfied that 'no firm dependence can ever be placed upon [the poligars'] allegiance or indeed on their obedience unless kept in awe by the presence of a military force—that it will always be better to pay them than to place power and influence and the means of mischief in their Hands'.[3] Whether in fact a policy in agreement with the views of the Court of Directors could have been a practical alternative to that of Munro seems doubtful: doubtful not only because of the unsettled conditions of the Ceded Districts, but because, one suspects, the Court's view of the poligars was not an entirely realistic one. This Munro suggested in a letter to Bentinck, when there was a possibility of the poligars' reinstatement, and his strictures were to a considerable extent justified.

Of the men who argue in favour of the Polligars [he wrote] it may be doubted whether any one individual rightly understands what Polligars are, or has ever seriously considered what would be the probable consequences of their reinstatement. They do not know that the Polligars of the Ceded Districts never were regarded as Landlords but as petty Princes ... that they were despised and detested by all the better classes of their subjects, and that as they can command no support but through the exercise of power they can never be converted into private Landowners who would devote their whole attention to the improvement of their Estates, but will always maintain bodies of armed men and endeavour as far as they can to act as petty Sovereigns. . . . it is not to be believed that such men if reinstated would ever ... become in anything like Country gentlemen which the term Zemindar has often erroneously been said to imply.[4]

The poligars of the Ceded Districts were not the only ones with whom Munro was concerned. In 1804-5 the western poligars of Arcot were in rebellion. After refusing to treat with the officer commanding the troops against them, rejecting the offers of government commissioners, and declining to meet the commissioner again for fear of their safety, their confidence in Munro was so high that they went to him, accepted his terms, and accompanied him to be turned over to Colonel Moneypenny.

While he was bringing the poligars to submission Munro also had regularly to collect the revenue. In his first year in the district the land revenue realised 1,006,693 pagodas [£402,637], or about one-third less than the value put upon the country when it was ceded to the Company. In his final year this had increased to 1,517,272 pagodas [£606,909], and in one year, 1805–6, when the season was extraordinarily favourable, had exceeded that amount by considerably more than a lakh of pagodas. For two years of the seven there were severe droughts, much of the land was left unsown, and many cattle perished from want of feed. Munro was forced to remit the revenue on much of the land; but while the revenue of the neighbouring districts fell by as much as one-half, in the Ceded Districts it fell only from about eighteen lakhs of pagodas to just under sixteen lakhs.

In addition to dealing with the poligars and collecting the revenue, Munro, from the end of 1802 when the alarm of a Maratha war began, until March 1805 was engaged in supplying grain and bullocks for the army in the field. He provided about 25,000 carriage bullocks, and 30,000 more were constantly employed during that period in carrying grain to the divisions in the field. It is hardly surprising that at one time he reported that he had more work than he could get through.

I have a constant correspondence with my own Amildar [he wrote] and an occasional one with those of other Divisions . . . and with many of the Inhabitants who have either disputes among themselves or Complaints against the Amildars. I find that it takes about three hours every day, to hear those letters and to dictate and hear when written the answers made to them. I give two hours every day to the hearing of complaints which are so numerous that that time is barely sufficient to enquire into them in a cursory manner. Five hours are therefore employed every day in the week on what constitutes but the smallest part of my business for I have besides this to look after the Native and English accounts to superintend the Settlements which occupy above seven months every year to qualify myself by investigation into the past and present state of the Country to judge what the Revenue ought to be for the present and how it may be augmented hereafter, to examine the charges against District and Village servants for peculation which are brought forward almost every day and to conduct the Survey.[1]

In appointing Munro to the Ceded Districts, Lord Clive hoped for an 'immediate and vigorous assertion of the Company's authority', as a foundation for 'an early establishment of a permanent system of Revenue and Judicature',[2]—a system the model for which he believed to be that established in Bengal by Cornwallis. The Company's authority, as we have seen, was firmly established. The zamindari settlement, however, was to be challenged in its basic ideas by Munro, and never extensively put into practice.

In the Ceded Districts Munro found, in contrast with Kanara, that all the land belonged to government—'the very name of private property in soil is unknown'[3]—and while the revenue was collected from the cultivators by the heads of villages these had no landed property in their villages beyond that of small inams which they were allowed to enjoy for acting as collectors. In his first revenue settlement, because of the late stage of the season and his preoccupation with establishing good order, Munro instructed his assistants to settle with these heads of villages, who were to be responsible individually for the rent of their own villages, and collectively for that of whole districts. They were to settle with the ryots in their village and could retain any surplus collected above the government assessment.[4] To make over villages and small estates to these men in perpetuity, Munro believed, could only endanger the future increase of the revenue because, doubting the stability of any tenure, their indigence would 'irresistibly urge them to take advantage of present possession and endeavour to enrich themselves by oppressing their Tenants'.[5] The only certain way of raising the revenue to its former standard was for government to retain in its own hands, for 'some years', the regulation of the assessment not only of villages and districts, but of every individual cultivator. If, however, in that period the arable land was all surveyed—as had been ordered by the Board of Revenue—and the rent of every field fixed, the farmers would acquire confidence in the government, the revenue would be increased and then the country could be divided into large estates without endangering its prosperity.[1]

In August 1801, the beginning of Munro's second revenue year in the Ceded Districts, he instructed his assistant collectors to make their settlements directly with every cultivator who paid rent to government. The cultivators were to be severally responsible for their rent, and they and the patel jointly for the rent of the whole village.[2] The assessment was regulated both by the quality of the land and the condition of the cultivator. The revenue was in money but was regulated by the 'supposed produce', and varied 'under different circumstances probably from two fifths to three fifths' of the produce.[3] In making such an annual settlement, Munro believed there were three methods which could be followed: to make a settlement with all the villages in a district at once, and only after having set the total assessments for them all to proceed to the individual settlement with every inhabitant of each village; to make the village settlement of one village and then the individual settlement of it before proceeding to another; or thirdly, to begin by settling with each individual of one village separately, and then by adding their rents together to make the village settlement.[4] The first way, which was the one used by Munro himself, had the advantage of being comparatively expeditious, and by assembling all the patels and curnums of a district in one place the variety of opinion and information was likely to produce a more accurate estimate of the value of each village, and the joint responsibility of the patels for the district revenue would make it difficult for any one of their number to conceal resources. After Munro had made the settlement with all the villages in his division, that with the individual cultivators was made by the amildar sent from the kachahri, a written agreement was made out for every ryot paying revenue, and this was sent to the kachahri to be signed by the collector. The difficulty with the second way, that of making the assessment of each village separately, was simply lack of time. With all the advantages of the collector being on the spot and able to view a disputed field or the state of a reservoir, the fact was that no collector, using such a method, could settle his division in the season. When the country had been surveyed, however, Munro wrote,

the individual supercedes both the village and district settlement, because it is then no longer necessary to waste time in endeavouring to persuade the cultivators to accede to the assessment. The rent of every field being fixed each cultivator takes or rejects what he pleases and the rents of all the fields occupied in the course of the year in any one village form what is called the settlement of that village.[1]

A survey of the Ceded Districts was begun in June 1802 and completed five years later at a cost of over 80,000 pagodas [£32,000]. When it was begun there were only four servants in Munro's kachahri who understood land measurement. As it went on more of the inhabitants were trained; by the end of the first year the number of surveyors amounted to fifty and in the following year reached one hundred. The survey was divided into two entirely separate parts; the measurement of the extent of land of all sorts—roads, sites of towns and villages, beds of reservoirs and rivers, wastes and jungles being included—and the assessment of an actual money rent on each field. Detailed written instructions were given to all concerned in the survey,[2] and at each stage the work was carefully checked. The patel and curnum with the other inhabitants attended while the surveyors worked in their village, and each ryot had notice of the time that his field was to be measured, in order that he might be present. To correct the measurement of the surveyors, head surveyors also were employed, who measured monthly one-tenth of the land fixed for a surveyor, tried the measurement of each surveyor every month, and if any ryot complained of the unfair measurement of his field measured it once more. The surveyors were followed by the assessors, who 'went over the land with the Potail, Curnums, and Ryots, and arranged it in different classes according to its quality'. The classification was in fact made 'rather by the Potail, Curnum, and Ryots, than by the Assessor; for he adopted their opinion, unless he saw evident cause to believe that it was wrong, when reference was made to the head Ryots of any of the neighbouring villages, who fixed the class to which the land in dispute should belong.'[1] Experience showed that if the sums assessed on each field were added up the aggregate sum was, in fact, greater than the district could easily realise. The whole classification and assessment, therefore, underwent a complete investigation at the collector's kachahri. All the patels, curnums and principal ryots were assembled and

the business was begun by fixing the sum which was to be the total revenue of the district. This was usually effected by the Collector in a few days, by comparing the collections under the native princes, under the Company's Government from its commencement, the estimates of the ordinary and head assessors, and the opinions of the most intelligent natives. ... The amount fixed by the Collector was usually from five to fifteen per cent. lower than the estimates of the assessors.[2]

The next stage was to decide what share of this remission should be granted to each of the villages in the district, and this was a last opportunity to check their relative assessments and also those of the different grades of land within them if there were still any complaints. Finally the revenue payable on each field was recorded. The survey was complete save for a check on those fields which during the first year had been claimed by their cultivators to be overrated, whereupon they were again examined in the presence of the leading inhabitants, and their rent either lowered or confirmed.

While Munro was pressing on with the survey and ryotwari settlement of the Ceded Districts, in other parts of the Presidency the Bengal system was introduced. Following the instructions for its adoption given by Wellesley in 1798, the Board of Revenue proposed that the best way of meeting the difficulty caused by the absence of zamindars was to group villages to form estates of convenient size, and sell them by auction to the highest bidder. The Bengal zamindars did perhaps bear enough resemblance to English landlords to support those advocates of the settlement who believed that they would make it their object to improve their estates. No one can have held out the same hopes in Madras. The purchasers of estates were not landlords but farmers of revenue, and in Madras support for the settlement was based not on the aim of improving and extending cultivation so much as of relieving government of the duty of assessing and collecting the land revenue, a duty which government officers were judged incompetent to perform. The Madras government accepted the Board's proposals, in 1802 a special commission for the permanent settlement of the land revenue was appointed,[1] and in two years the Northern Sirkars, the Jagir, the Baramahal and Dindigul were settled on the lines recommended. Simultaneously with the introduction of the zamindari system in each district came a new judicial system and a code of regulations modelled on those of Bengal. A district judge and magistrate was appointed who took over the civil and criminal jurisdiction formerly exercised by the collector; and under him, as magistrate, was placed the new police force of thanadars and daroghas. As in Bengal the new courts and new regulations were intended to protect the cultivators' rights against the landlord whom the zamindari settlement had placed over them, as well as to protect the zamindar against the government and its servants. In this they failed, and for the same reasons as in Bengal: fettered by British rules of procedure and evidence, litigation proved to be so lengthy and tedious a business that protection through the courts was quite illusory.

This was certainly not realised at first. Wellesley's enthusiasm for a 'distribution of legislative, executive, and judicial powers of the state, analogous to that which forms the basis of the British constitution', and his anxiety to see these constitutional principles adopted in the Madras territories, were such that he maintained that the question of a permanent settlement of the land revenue was altogether separate, and formed no necessary part of the 'fundamental principle of the new constitution', and that the introduction of the new judicial system could, in fact, precede the permanent settlement.[1] There were two difficulties in the way of this. The first, which Munro was to emphasise, was that the full establishment of the judicial system, with its lengthy and involved procedure, was likely to hold up the conclusion of the revenue settlement. The second was that the 'new constitution' pivoted on the definition and enforcement of private property rights in the western sense.[2] Lord William Bentinck, who on 30 August 1803 at the age of twenty-nine had succeeded Lord Clive as Governor of Madras and whose youth was paralleled by a vigour and ability in marked contrast to his predecessor,[3] was inclined to agree with Wellesley.

I have paid a great deal of attention to the Revenue Management in this country [he wrote to Castlereagh] .... my opinion is that we have rode the country too hard and the consequence is, that it is in a state of most lamentable poverty. Great oppression is I fear exercised too generally in the Collection of the Revenues. ... I believe the service to be very honourable but they have been accustomed to arbitrary Government. ... Where is the man to be found sufficiently virtuous not to abuse it? ... The conviction upon my mind of the certainty of these abuses made me urge the Governor-General to permit the general introduction of Courts of Justice through the Districts under this Presidency whether the permanent settlement had taken place or not. ... it is a perfect fact, that ... with all our benevolence and humanity ... the administration of Justice has been completely neglected.[4]

Such a proposal was strongly opposed by Munro. That the country was in a state of 'lamentable poverty' he agreed; but in his view a permanent settlement of the revenue was of far greater importance in improving the country than the introduction of courts, and so far as the new judicial system proved a check on concluding the settlements it would be a bad thing.[1] The introduction of the new regulations, 'evidently framed for a country permanently assessed', into one where the revenue was settled annually in detail might so 'embarrass the Collector with the observance of forms', Munro argued, 'that he would never be able to effect a permanent settlement', which was in fact the quickest way of placing the great body of the inhabitants in the 'enjoyment of a real and defined property'.[2] Indeed even before the revenue settlement was begun in newly acquired country, order must be established, the powers of any zamindars and poligars likely to disturb the peace must be reduced, and this could be better done in the beginning by a single person, entrusted with extraordinary powers, than afterwards by magistrates when the country was divided into zillahs. The separation of civil and judicial powers, Munro wrote, was not the indigenous system, and 'whatever excellence such a system may possess it can never be supposed that the mere want of a thing which has never been heard of by the natives shall drive them to insurrection'. The 'present happy state of Bengal', he suggested, was less owing to the introduction of the new judicial system than to the establishment of permanent rents, and to the long enjoyment of profound peace.

No doubt can exist with respect to the beneficial influence which the new form of Gov[t]. will have upon the Country—but as it must for a long time be little understood by the great mass of the inhabitants its effects must be slow and almost imperceptible. The advantage of a fixed rent on the Country is immediate and as easily comprehended by the meanest cultivator. The distress which a temporary assess[t]. whether for one year or a short period of years produces every season among the under Farmers far outweighs all the advantages that can be expected in the same time from the Courts of Justice—a permanent rent would go further in one year in promoting the improvement of the country and the comfort of the Inhabitants than the Courts of Justice in Twenty.[3]

The Board of Revenue, having been instructed by the Governor in Council to propose an arrangement for dividing into zillahs the districts not permanently settled, and to frame a regulation for the future collection of the revenue on the principles of that introduced into the Ceded Provinces of Oudh, proposed that in conformity with the principle of forming a general rent for a term of years, the lands should either be rented out to zamindars or, where they did not exist, be formed into leasehold estates and the leases disposed of by auction. If neither of these was possible a ryotwari settlement should be formed.[1] The recommendations drawn up by the Board were sent to all the collectors in the Presidency for their comments. Munro criticised what he viewed as unjustified changes from local practice, particularly the proposal to deprive the patel of his 'rank, influence, and privileges' by reducing him from 'the station of chief of the village to that of a common cultivator' under the man who bid most for the lease of the estate.[2] The new system, Munro wrote,

while it endeavours to establish a permanent proprietory right in land . . . ought not to annihilate the rights of the most numerous body of landholders in the Country, or to erect new Estates by sweeping away the old ones. . . . The Potails it may be said have the option of retaining their Estates, but it is by purchasing them, and by offering more than any stranger for what is already their own. Instead therefore of selling the leases it would be better to grant them to the Potails.[3]

On the kind of permanent settlement that should ultimately be made Munro did not, at this time, express any definite views. For the Ceded Districts, however, he urged that until the survey was completed there should be a ryotwari settlement, because no other could be introduced 'without great interruption to the Survey'— either the survey or the forming of a lease being sufficient to occupy all of his time.[4] In a private letter to William Petrie,[5] the president of the Board, he put it more strongly:

There is something extravagant [he wrote] in the precipitation with which the Bengal Government urge forward this measure [the permanent settlement]. They hurry great Provinces off their hands as if they were private Estates long before they can form any judgment of what they are worth. . . . the moment that the Country is divided into Estates the door of investigation is compleatly shut. It is really an extraordinary method of proceeding—first to deprive yourself of the means of acquiring information, and then to sit gravely down to pursue your research.[1]

The Board of Revenue took the same view as Munro,[2] and Bentinck decided that the proposed regulations should not be extended to the unsettled districts of the Presidency, but the existing forms of management should continue until the survey and assessments were completed.[3] Believing this to be 'one of the most important questions that [had] ever come before the consideration of Government', he travelled to Calcutta to impress his argument on the Supreme Government.[4] The Board of Revenue had also urged that the courts of justice could not be introduced into unsettled districts without obstructing the 'acquirement of that accurate knowledge of the resources of the Country which can form the only basis of an equitable assessment, whether permanent or temporary';[5] on this question, however, Bentinck believed the Supreme Government had left the Madras Government no discretion. They had ordered the introduction of the courts; indeed Bentinck 'entirely' agreed in their opinion,[6] and during 1806 the courts were introduced into those districts still unsettled. When the survey and assessment had been completed and a permanent settlement could be made, however, Bentinck proposed that where the lands had not been disposed of the ryots should be confirmed 'in possession of their lands in perpetuity upon a fixed rent without any intermediate agent between the Government and the Ryot'.[7] This would, in fact, be making permanent the ryotwari system put into practice by Munro in the Ceded Districts.

The creation of zamindars, where none before existed, in Bentinck's view was 'neither calculated to improve the condition of the lower orders of the people, nor politically wise, with reference to the future security' of the government. In recording his proposal for making the ryotwari annual settlement, 'from which such vast advantage [had] been derived', the basis of the permanent settlement, he asked that William Thackeray should be released from his position as judge in Masulipatam for six months to assist him in his investigations.[1] Thackeray had worked under Munro in the Ceded Districts from 1800 to 1803, and the memoir which he prepared for Bentinck in favour of 'Ryotwar Permanent Settlements'[2] followed closely Munro's arguments for such a settlement.[3] Thackeray's conclusions strengthened Bentinck's conviction against a zamindari settlement: Bentinck's support for a ryotwari system did not, he himself believed, represent a departure from the basic principle of the permanent settlement—which in his view was the limitation of the demands of the sarkar—but rather a change in the details of the operation of the scheme.[4]

After having decided in favour of a ryotwari settlement, Bentinck learned of the 'exact nature of the tenures of land in Canara', which, he believed, demonstrated to a remarkable degree the conditions he hoped such a settlement would produce.[5] 'The great distinction between a Rayet in [the Ceded Districts] and in Canara', Munro had told him, 'is that here he regards himself as an annual tenant and there as a Landlord.'[6] In Kanara Bentinck saw a land tax defined in its amount and equally distributed; every man knew his exact obligations to the sarkar and was 'assured of the quiet enjoyment of the surplus produce of his labour', and the poor were secure against extra assessments from the head inhabitants. From these circumstances arose the true encouragement to industry: cultivation increased, and the revenue was easily realised. With such a picture—based largely on Munro's two reports of 1800—it is not surprising that Bentinck recorded his 'satisfaction in finding theory reduced to practice, and speculation proved by the most successful experiments. Canara thus became the great land-mark by which I hoped to trace out those principles and regulations which might be applicable to the unsettled districts, where permanent tenures are to be introduced.'[7]

In October 1806 Bentinck appointed Thackeray a member of

the Board of Revenue, and expressed at the time his view that only the importance of Munro's work in the Ceded Districts prevented his appointment to fill the vacancy.[1] Bentinck recognised Munro's knowledge of revenue and administrative questions as being virtually unrivalled in the Presidency. 'I believe the only Principal Collectors really deserving of that title are Col. Munro and Mr Wallace',[2] he had written to Petrie,[3] and the 'information and advice of... Munro' he considered 'to be essential and indispensable to the trial and ultimate adoption' of any plan of settlement which his enquiries led him to prepare.[4]

Munro himself, in a long letter to the Board of Revenue, dated 25 August 1805, came out strongly in favour of a ryotwari settlement, not only while the survey was in progress, but following its completion, as the basis of a permanent system.[5] Two years later, when the survey was completed, he reiterated his case in a report which in its clarity, its comprehensiveness, and not least, its brevity, stood alone in the mass of writing called forth by the discussions taking place at Fort St George.[6] These two reports amount to far more than a plan for a system of revenue settlement: they reflect both Munro's experience and his conservatism in his emphasis that the social habits and political institutions existing in the districts should form the basis of any revenue settlement or judicial system. It was not the conservatism, however, of stubborn ignorance or of self-satisfied vested interest, but of informed sympathy, of a paternalism both autocratic and Romantic.

When a country falls under the dominion of a foreign power, Munro wrote, 'it is usually found to be the wisest plan to leave it in possession of its own laws and customs, and to endeavour rather to ameliorate than to abolish them and substitute others in their room'.[7] His investigation of the system of landed property and tenures which had always prevailed in India indicated to him that the sovereign had at all times been regarded as the sole landlord, and that the country had been divided into an immense number of small farms held immediately of the sovereign by their cultivators.

There was no description of landholders similar to the owners of estates whom it had been proposed to create.[1] A settlement directly with the cultivators, as that which had always been followed, was therefore 'best adapted to the manners and prejudices of the inhabitants'. There were practical arguments in favour of such a settlement, arguments used first by Munro when he was in the Baramahal, and confirmed for him by his experience in Kanara. The patels of villages and the principal cultivators, who in the absence of a zamindari class were the only people likely to become owners of estates, had never heard of private landed property, or of any landlord but the state. It would be almost impossible, he considered, to persuade them that government had transferred its right in the soil to them:

nothing but the experience of a great number of years would convince them that they were actually its proprietors. They would therefore, as long as they entertained doubts of the stability of their tenures act as if they were in daily expectation of a change. They would endeavour to make the most of their Estates while in their possession, they would press heavy on the Ryots and they would not employ much stock, even if they had it in improvements.... As they are in general as poor as the common Cultivators they could make no advances from their own funds, neither is it probable that they would make any from the remission which Government might deem it adviseable to make in order to secure the permanency of the settlement.[2]

Less than ten years after this was written such a position did come about, when the Board of Revenue adopted a policy of village settlements and, in effect, tried to turn the patels into minor zamindars.[3]

Munro thought that a ryotwari settlement had the advantages of being the system which had always prevailed in India, and of being the one into which all others would eventually resolve themselves.[4] It was more simple (once the survey was completed) than the zamindari plan, and, he believed, it would produce a quieter and more law-abiding population than the establishment of holders of large estates. It was better calculated to promote industry and augment the produce of the country, because it would create more proprietors. The ryot would be more likely to improve his land as a proprietor than as a tenant of a zamindar. As well as being more immediately interested in the cultivation of his fields, the small proprietor would be a better manager and farmer than the great one, would take greater pains, and produce a more abundant crop. Should a remission be made in the assessment, it would, under a ryotwari settlement, go directly to the cultivator and the whole of it would immediately be applied to the improvement of the country. By allowing the revenue to increase or diminish each year according to the extent of cultivation, failures would become less frequent and the increase of agricultural stock would be accelerated, and this without occasioning, on an average of years, any loss to government. The fluctuation would decrease steadily as the ryots became wealthier. Finally the ryotwari system, by retaining in the hands of government all unoccupied lands—unlike the zamindari settlement where such land was included in the estates—gave it the power of gradually augmenting the revenue, without imposing any fresh burden upon the ryots, as long as there was an acre of waste in the country.[1]

The ultimate object, Munro held, in making a direct settlement with the ryots the permanent arrangement in the Ceded Districts, 'should be the rendering the Cultivators stationary, the lands saleable, and the farms small Estates—but', he added, 'this can only be effected by making such an abatement of rent as shall leave to the Cultivator after discharging all demands such a profit as may enable him to find a purchaser whenever he may wish to dispose of his farm.'[2] It was not to be supposed that land would become saleable immediately on the reduction of rent, but it would become so gradually in the course of twenty or twenty-five years, and this object could be attained if the government rent was fixed at the equivalent to one-third the value of the crop grown upon the land.

If the ryot were allowed to enjoy the remainder and all such future increase as might arise from his industry, he would never relinquish his farm, and all cultivated land would soon become private landed property. If more than one-third is demanded as rent, there can be no private landed property; for it is found that when land which has formerly been enam, is assessed, that as long as the rate is not more than one-third of the produce, the land is regarded as a private estate, and can generally be sold; but that whenever the rate exceeds one-third, the land is scarcely ever saleable, is no longer reckoned private property, and is often abandoned.[1]

The existing assessment of the Ceded Districts Munro estimated to be about 45 per cent of the gross produce. To bring it down to the one-third, without which reduction the land could never become saleable, nor any permanent settlement be made calculated to improve the condition of the ryots or of the public revenue, required a remission of 25 per cent in the assessment, and this Munro recommended to the Board. The loss to revenue, moreover, would not be as great as that, as the reduction was not to be made on the average of former collections, but on the survey assessment, which never had been completely realised; and unlike the revenue from a zamindari settlement, which in ten years time would be exactly the same amount, the ryotwari settlement should produce a steady increase in revenue as cultivation expanded.

The principles on which Munro proposed the permanent settlement should be made were few and simple, the most important being:

1st. The settlement shall be ryotwary.

2nd. The amount of the settlement shall increase and decrease annually, according to the extent of the land in cultivation.

3rd. A reduction of twenty-five per cent. on all land shall be made in the survey rate of assessment.

4th. An additional reduction in the assessment of eight per cent., or thirty-three per cent. in all, shall be allowed on all lands watered by wells, or by water raised by machinery from rivers ... provided the cultivators keep the wells or embankments ... in repair at their own expense. A similar reduction shall be allowed on the lands watered by small tanks, wherever the cultivators agree to bear the expense of repairs.

5th. Every Ryot shall be at liberty, at the end of every year, to throw up a part of his land, or to occupy more, according to his circumstances; but whether he throw up or occupy, shall not be permitted to select, but shall take or reject proportional shares of the good and bad together.

6th. Every Ryot, as long as he pays the rent of his land, shall be considered as the complete owner of the soil, and shall be at liberty to let it to a tenant without any hesitation as to rent and to sell it as he pleases.

7th. No remission shall be made, on ordinary occasions, for bad crops or other accidents. Should failures occur, which cannot be made good from the property or land of the defaulters, the villages in which they happen shall be liable for them, to the extent of ten per cent. additional on the rent of the remaining Ryots, but no further.

8th. All unoccupied land shall remain in the hands of Government, and the rent of whatever part of it may be hereafter cultivated shall be added to the public revenue.[1]

Whatever mode of settlement was finally adopted, however, the inhabitants, in Munro's view, would 'suffer great inconvenience, and even distress, from the judicial regulations' if they were not amended.[2] The evils, which were likely to increase rather than diminish, were 'delay, vexation, bribery, wrong decisions'. The delay arose from the forms of proceeding which not only the European judge but the native commissioners were required to adhere to, and from the great proportion of suits, even of the most petty nature, which were brought before the zillah judge. The number of causes undecided at any moment gave an inadequate indication of the extent of this delay; for as great a number might be held back and never brought into court at all, from the parties despairing of ever getting them adjusted there. 'Justice can hardly be said to be administered', Munro wrote, 'when it proceeds so slowly as not to keep pace, in any degree, with the demands of the country.' By bringing every suit before a European judge erroneous decisions were increased, for no judge 'however intelligent he may be [can] be half so well qualified as a native jury to appreciate the characters of parties and witnesses, and to distinguish between true and false evidence'. And yet the native munsiffs or commissioners, for whom provision was made in the judicial code, were so restricted, and their proceedings so liable to be suspended or reversed, that the effect was to centre the whole administration of civil justice in the person of the European zillah judge. If there was no complete remedy for these evils, it was clear to Munro—as he had first become convinced in the Baramahal—that in India, as in any populous country, justice could be 'properly distributed only by means of the natives'. The most effectual reform would be to make use of the native panchayat, or jury, which Munro reported as 'the only mode of trial which is general and popular' among the inhabitants.

No native [he wrote] thinks that justice is done where [the case is not decided by panchayat]; and in appeals of causes formerly settled, whether under a native government or under that of the Company, previous to the establishment of courts, the reason assigned in almost every instance was, that the decision was not given by a punchayet but by a public officer, or by persons acting under his influence or sitting in his presence. The native who has a good cause, always applies for a punchayet; while he who has a bad one seeks the decision of a Collector or a Judge, because he knows it is easier to deceive them.[1]

Before Munro's report had been considered by the government instructions were received from the Court of Directors removing Bentinck as governor, and in 1808 the Board of Revenue decided that instead of working along the lines of the ryotwari system, they should once again experiment with village leases. The Board was strongly influenced by John Hodgson,[2] one of its members, whose experience as a collector had been in the Jagir. There he found in each village a body of mirasdars, or landholders, whose claim to a permanent proprietory right in land rested on a tradition of joint colonisation of the village. The revenue settlement there was made by the leading mirasdars settling with the revenue officers on behalf of the village. This village system, Hodgson persuaded his colleagues, might be made the foundation of a satisfactory land revenue system for the whole presidency. Where there were no mirasdars to be found—as in the Ceded Districts—the lease could be given to the village headman. The belief of Hodgson's that such a settlement would keep alive and stimulate the village institutions of self-government was not the only motive leading to its adoption (nor was it in fact to be justified by subsequent developments); it was also held that the village settlement would be more economical than the ryotwari system, and would overcome the difficulties placed in the way of realising the revenue under a ryotwari system by the introduction of the judicial code.[1]

Munro had recommended an immediate reduction of 25 per cent in the assessment of the Ceded Districts if the ryotwari settlement was to be made permanent. But, as Thackeray wrote:

so far from granting remissions [government] wanted money. In the settled Districts, the Revenue could not be raised: there was therefore reason to fear the Rayets in the unsettled would be worse not better off. If the Courts had not been established, they would have been plundered: but, as the system of restrictions and compulsion had been destroyed, there was a great danger of considerable loss of Revenue. Rayetwari could not be carried on without a remission. Government then could not afford a remission. In such circumstances, a village-rent on just principles was, perhaps, the only plan that could be pursued with success.[2]

The impediments to the ready realisation of the revenue directly from the ryots under the new judicial system were in consequence of its being required by law, that in the settlement of disputes respecting land revenue payments, and in recovering arrears due, the same formal process had to be gone through, however small the amount. It was believed that this difficulty could be avoided by throwing the responsibility of assessing and collecting the dues of each cultivator on to the villagers themselves who held the lease. At the same time it was argued that the new judicial system provided a safeguard for protecting the rights of the other ryots in the village from oppressive and corrupt action by the leaseholding mirasdars or patels, abuses of power which at an earlier date had seemed the inevitable result of village settlements.

From the government's point of view, and indeed from practically any other, the village system was not a success: whatever its theoretical advantages, it was in practice no more able than a ryotwari settlement to produce a revenue which, as later became clear, was assessed at a rate considerably higher than the country could bear. A. D. Campbell,[1] who as secretary of the Board of Revenue had at first supported the system strongly, later told a committee of the House of Commons:

generally . . . a few only of the villagers entered into the lease, and thus stood as temporary middlemen between the government and the rest of the country. The inferior ryots were shut out from all immediate communication with the government officers, oppressed by their more powerful brethren the renters, who in good seasons pocketed all the profits, and in bad cast upon them, by extra assessments, or saddling them with waste land, the greater burden of the leases; so that at the expiration of the 10 years the villages generally returned into the hands of government in a lamentable state of impoverishment, and in some districts . . . of absolute bankruptcy.[2]

As far as future administrative policy in Madras was concerned, however, the exact results of the village settlements were of little importance. In the six years following their introduction the home government was led to take an interest in the administration of its Indian possessions. A policy was evolved which owed more to Munro than to the ideas of the 'presidency men' in Madras; and when Munro returned to India in 1814 after six years at home, it was to put into effect the administrative system which had become known by his name.

CHAPTER 4

THE HOME GOVERNMENT, 1808–14

Munro returned to England on leave in the beginning of 1808, and it has been written that his stay there 'gradually converted both the Court of Directors and the Board of Control to his own views'.[1] Certainly by the time he returned to India in 1814 they shared those views, but their conversion was not as straightforward a matter as this seems to suggest. Before there was any chance of Munro's views gaining support it was clear that there would have to be doubts as to the wisdom of the Cornwallis system as a system, and not just as to the success with which it was being put into practice. And, as one Director wrote, 'the reverence entertained for its illustrious founder, whose pure and benevolent motives never were, and probably never will be disputed, proved in this Country especially a powerful support to the system, and induced a ready belief on insufficient grounds, that everything was going right until irresistible evidence forced itself forward to show that almost everything had been wrong.'[2] This evidence was brought forward by the Committee of the House of Commons which in the years 1810–12 carried out an investigation into the system of government in India, the first such investigation since 1782, and one of a series of enquiries into different aspects of the Company's activities caused by the imminence of the decision on the renewal of its Charter. 'It seems no strained position', wrote a critic of the Cornwallis system in 1817, 'to assume that the sufferings of our Indian subjects might to this day have been unknown here, even among those who feel a real interest in their welfare, had not the Committee of the House of Commons . . . led the way to free enquiry into their actual state.'[3]

The Committee called in to assist them Samuel Davis, elected a Director of the Company in 1810, who had not long before returned from Bengal determined 'to unmask the effects of Lord Cornwallis's Code'.[1] Robert Dundas, the President of the Board, referred him to James Cumming, the head of the Board's Revenue and Judicial Department, to be supplied with such official records as he might need. Cumming did more than supply records; his ability and unrivalled knowledge of administrative affairs were quickly apparent, and on Davis's suggestion the Committee agreed that Davis should confine himself to writing that part of the report relating to the Bengal territories, while Cumming prepared that on Madras.[2] Cumming was able to do this partly because in 1807 the Board had been reorganised: its old division into departments dealing with each Presidency had been replaced by departments dealing with particular subjects. Before this date 'neither the president nor the members, still less the permanent officers of the Board, had any detailed knowledge of what was going on in the several departments of India, or took any concern in matters which did not excite the attention of Parliament or the public.'[3] After the reorganisation revenue and judicial affairs gained a share of the attention which had formerly been largely devoted to political and strategic questions.

From about 1801 Cumming, 'in order to qualify [himself] for being a more useful functionary to the Board'[4] had devoted 'many of [his] leisure hours' to the investigation of the revenue and judicial records; while his official services amounted to no more 'than copying papers when required, making indexes to the public dispatches, and abstracts of their contents which are rarely or never read by the Board'.[5] The first result of the rearrangement of the office was that Cumming was 'left unmolested to copy papers and pursue [his] own private studies'[6] until 1811, when Thomas Wallace, a member of the Board and chairman of the Committee of the House of Commons which was to produce the *Fifth Report*, having accidentally heard of Cumming's studies, sought his views on the state of things in the Judicial Department. This was the first interview Cumming had ever had with a Commissioner of the

Board.[1] Following it he wrote his 'Memoir on the Revision of the Judicial System under the Government of Fort St George ...',[2] one of a series of memoirs which are still impressive for their marshalling of fact and clear argument. Apart from Wallace the Board ignored the subject: at this time the initiative was being taken by the House of Commons committee. Munro had sent Dundas a paper of his own on the Madras judicial system[3] without arousing interest. Most of Dundas's time and energy were spent in drawn-out negotiations with the Directors over the renewal of the Company's Charter, and it was only with the appointment of the new Board in 1812 that there was any interest in administration.

Cumming saw little to support in the Cornwallis system, and favoured a ryotwari settlement and the supremacy of the executive over the judicial arm of government—a system which would, he believed, have the twin virtues of preserving native practice, and saving government money. The ryotwari system had been superseded not because it was bad in itself: the Boards of Revenue of successive administrations at Fort St George had recognised its virtues and authorised its extension to every district which did not present obstacles to the measure; the 'ablest and most experienced Collectors were the most forward and earnest, in recording their sentiments in favour of the system'.[4] It was given up, Cumming believed, because the decision had been made to introduce the Bengal judicial regulations: this code was in some respects incompatible with a ryotwari settlement,[5] and the latter was therefore abandoned. Cumming, like Munro, believed this to be quite the wrong way out of the difficulty. For the judicial code, to which the ryotwari system had been sacrificed, was itself open to considerable criticism, on the grounds of its expense and inefficiency. The only effectual way in which the demands for justice could be met, Cumming wrote, was to

transfer the greater part of the business, now conducted by the Zillah Courts, to the hands of respectable and intelligent natives, who would discharge the duty on so much smaller a salary than the Zillah Judges that the means of administering

Justice might be enlarged to the necessary extent: and yet more than one third the expence attending the present Establishments, be saved to the Company: while the measure would be acceptable to the Natives, as a return to that mode of Judiciary administration to which they had been habituated.[1]

Not only would the measure 'be acceptable to the Natives' but it would be more efficient, as no European could be so well qualified to dispense justice as an Indian. The great argument against giving Indians any extensive judicial authority was their reputed proneness to corruption, and although, Cumming wrote, it had to be admitted that they were 'more liable to abuse the use of power than European servants',[2] this could be largely attributed to the lack of an efficient system of check and control, and to that 'rapacious spirit' of the 'Mahomedan Governments, which considered power only as the instrument of obtaining wealth'. A great increase in the number of Indians employed in the judicial service might mean that justice would be 'administered in a less regular manner but it would be administered more readily, more promptly: and on the whole more satisfactorily.'[3]

This alone was not enough. The forms of judicial proceeding, as well as the men administering them, needed to be changed, and to be simplified.[4] The difficulty of the Indians in understanding the nature and meaning of the regulations meant that they could not conduct and plead their own causes—although the regulations allowed them the option of doing so—but were dependent on professional pleaders, or vakils, who were held to be, in general, 'exceedingly illiterate', and accused of 'promoting litigation, by holding forth false hopes and promises of success to the clients'.[5] The strongest objection, however, to the process and rules of the courts was the delay caused in the dispatch of business. The number of undetermined suits in the zillah courts of Madras on 31 December 1808 was 31,842. The steps taken for reducing arrears—the appointment of assistant judges, an increase in the powers of registrars and munsiff commissioners—had all been tried in Bengal for several years before the same date, when the arrears there were 121,453: a number, the Court stated, 'they believed to be unprecedented in the Judicial Courts of any civilized Government'.[1] Cumming also believed that the panchayat should be used to settle many cases. He had been 'informed by Colonel Munro', he wrote, 'that in cases of dispute which he had enquired into, and which he had afterwards referred to a Punchayet, he almost always found, where his own opinion was different from that of the Punchayet that theirs was right and his own wrong'.[2]

In all these views Cumming was in full agreement with Munro, whom he described as a 'man of uncommon sagacity of mind, and uncommon knowledge of every subject connected with Indian Government',[3] and as 'one who has probably had a closer and more extensive intercourse with the natives of India, and has had better opportunities of practically investigating the nature of their Institutions, than any other person'.[4] Munro's final report on the settlement of the Ceded Districts, in which he had advocated a ryotwari settlement, contained, Cumming wrote, 'a juster and more able and practical argument on the subject compressed within an extraordinary narrow compass than can perhaps find its parralel [sic] in Indian Correspondence'.[5] He met Munro, sought his advice, submitted his own memoirs to him for his comments,[6] and quoted largely from Munro's reports, which indeed had the virtue, uncommon among the work of Indian administrators, of being ably written and comparatively brief. Whether Munro converted Cumming to his views, or whether Munro's experience merely confirmed Cumming in conclusions he had already reached, it is impossible to say. But Cumming's grasp of a well-considered alternative plan, added to his informed criticism of the Bengal system, enabled him to make the *Fifth Report* of the Committee of the House of Commons a landmark in Indian administration. The extraordinary thing is how far it was a matter of chance that his knowledge was drawn on, Wallace hearing of his work only a few months before the committee began its deliberations.[7] Without Cumming many of Munro's ideas would still probably have been eventually put into practice—they were after all shared to a greater or less extent by several of his contemporaries[1]—but not for some years, and not with the same coherence and forcefulness.

Although ostensibly a factual account of the revenue management of the Madras territories, that part of the *Fifth Report* written by Cumming presented a strong case for the ryotwari system, as opposed to those preceding and succeeding it; a case perhaps the more persuasive in not being explicitly argued.[2] From an examination of the effects, the Committee concluded that the ryotwari settlements had 'greatly improved the situation of the cultivator, by limiting the ... public assessment, according to his ability to satisfy it; by relieving him from the oppressive exactions of the native revenue officers, and securing him in the protection of his property and rights'.[3] This favourable change in their condition, the Committee believed, gave the ryots confidence in the Company's government, confidence increased by ready and direct contact between the inhabitants and the representatives of government; and with a new incentive to industry, cultivation had been extended and revenue increased without raising the level of the assessment. With these advantages it was a 'matter of regret, that any circumstances should have existed, to render the abandonment of ryotwar settlements necessary',[4] and, the Committee agreed, the light thrown on 'local institutions, and the Hindoo system of Financial economy' by the active and intelligent investigations of the Company's servants, rendered it highly expedient that the system of permanent settlement of the revenue 'should be reconsidered in its principles, before it be applied to provinces into which it has not yet been introduced, with a view to such modifications and improvements of it, as the more intimate practical knowledge we now possess of the local concerns of the country, may render desirable to be adopted'.[5]

After the publication of the *Fifth Report* in 1812 the new views rapidly gained support. Robert Dundas had been succeeded as

President of the Board in April 1812 by the Earl of Buckingham-shire, who in the 1790's had been Governor of Madras at the time of Read's first ryotwari settlements in the Baramahal. He was assisted by his brother-in-law, John Sullivan, who was considered 'a disciple of Thomas Munro',[1] and whose time was 'almost constantly devoted to researches connected with the Civil and political government of India'.[2] For four years the Board was to give Cumming every support. The first result was the Revenue Despatch to Madras of 16 December 1812, which ordered a ryotwari settlement in those districts not otherwise settled. That the revenue measure came before the judicial reforms is not surprising. At a time when the financial condition of the Company was far from flourishing, the ryotwari settlement advocated by Cumming and Munro found support also because the detailed surveys which were the first step in the settlement would reveal clearly, it was hoped, the taxable resources of the country. Lord Minto certainly discerned in the Directors 'a desire to avoid repeating in other territories the act of self denial which had been forced on them in Bengal'.[3]

Although the initiative had been taken by the Board the Court of Directors at last came out positively for the new system. After firmly ordering Munro back to India on several occasions—his three years leave having elapsed—they suddenly changed their minds and gave him permission to stay another year.[4] The reason seems to have been that, following the Parliamentary report, the Court intended to set up special committees of their own to investi-gate all aspects of the Company's activities. Munro, together with other prominent servants of the Company then in England, was called upon for information by the committee on revenue and judicial affairs, and 'his authority appears to have principally guided the Special Committee in their reasoning and conclusions on this momentous subject'.[5]

Why were the Court so slow to grasp the fact that their admini-strative system in India needed urgent attention—that, for example, the arrears in the business of the courts were so great that, Malcolm concluded, 'thousands appeal to our courts to evade not to obtain justice'?[1] One reason has already been mentioned: the extraordinary regard for Cornwallis which 'rendered it a species of political heresy to doubt the wisdom and expediency of his enactments'.[2] With this went the fact that of those Directors who had served in India (and there were several of them) the majority had been there when the Cornwallis system was virtually untried, when it stood for a new and hopeful way to peace, justice and prosperity. The outstanding exception was, of course, Davis. Like most men they based their views on their experience, rather than on later reports which might suggest a different picture. Yet to see what was really happening they would have had to read between the lines of the lengthy letters home, in which, on the whole, the Supreme Government appeared either as panegyrist of its own measures, or apologist for their failure in such a way that it generally found something to commend. 'When the operation of the Regulations proved adverse to their expectations in one respect, in another something had occurred to console them for the disappointment, by showing that some different but equally desirable end had been attained.'[3] Added to this difficulty was the fact that the Court appeared unable to keep up with the growing amount of correspondence. On 30 September 1808 there were 1,027 Revenue Paragraphs and 404 Judicial Paragraphs from Madras unanswered, and the numbers were rapidly increasing.[4] This being so it was hardly surprising that extra papers tended to be overlooked completely. In 1801 Wellesley, in order to discover the practical effects of the Cornwallis judicial system, had circulated a set of queries to the judges of Bengal. By the beginning of 1803 the replies to these queries were among the records in Leadenhall Street, and there they lay quietly, 'unread and unnoticed', until in 1811 Cumming brought them to the attention of Davis, who used them when he was preparing the Bengal section of the *Fifth Report*.[5]

The answers were called for by the Board afterwards [wrote Cumming], and when the 5th Report had made its appearance and while the Renewal of the Charter was under Parliamentary discussion they were ordered to be printed by the House of Commons, on the motion of some member. They have certainly had considerable effect in opening the eyes of the governing authorities at home to what has been the effect of the internal arrangements introduced into Bengal by Lord Cornwallis in the year 1793 and if they had not been suffered to sleep, for so many years among the public records of the East India Company, it is highly probable that they would have led to further enquiries and have thus been the means of taking more timely measures for applying a remedy, or at least of endeavouring to apply one to great political disorders and failures, in the administration of Indian affairs.[1]

While the Court of Directors failed to have any firm grasp of the difficulties of governing the vast area under their control, it cannot be said that Parliament was notably better informed. Until the publication of the *Fifth Report* there was no parliamentary mention of the administrative problems arising from the Corn-wallis system in Bengal, or created by the accession of new territory in the south of India. When the renewal of the Charter was discussed during the summer of 1813, the motions before Parliament did not directly touch on the administrative system; and had it not been for the speech of Robert Rickards, it is probable that nothing more would have been uttered on administration than the customary pious tributes to the character of Cornwallis, to its 'unsullied purity, great perseverance ... warm philanthropy [and] loftiness of spirit',[2] and to his 'wise and exemplary administration', which had 'tended so much to the prosperity, glory, honour, and advantage of the subjects in India'.[3]

Rickards had spent over twenty years in the west of India.[4] While acknowledging that the resolutions before the House did not touch on the subject, he spoke at length on the condition of the people of India, the state of its internal government, 'and the means of increasing the comforts, happiness, and security of the people'— compared with which, he judged, 'all other points of the question ... sink into insignificance'.[5] The benefits which the zamindari system might have contributed to this end were counteracted by the exorbitance of the assessment: and the judicial regulations which had accompanied the Cornwallis settlement, by the delays they caused in settling suits, had exacerbated the distress of the inhabitants, reducing the 'most ancient families from a state of influence and respectability to heavy distress, beggary, and ruin'. The extension of the Bengal revenue and judicial system to Madras had been shown in the *Fifth Report* to have been a 'pretty general failure'; though, Rickards added, under a more moderate assessment 'the zemindary system would certainly possess some advantages'. Under all the revenue systems lately adopted the condition of the ryot had been nearly the same, the universal poverty sprang from the same cause of excessive taxation; the denial to the cultivator of the 'fruits of honest labour', and of security for its enjoyment, was the cause of the widespread prevalence of violence and robbery, in combating which 'additional legal severities [would] only add to the cruelty and ferocity of those, whose necessities impel them to prey on the public'. To his description of widespread failure and misery Rickards made one remarkable exception: a district where, 'through the discernment and vigilance of a distinguished collector', the revenue was increased in eight years from ten to eighteen lakhs of star pagodas, chiefly by reducing the tax from nearly one-half to one-third of the gross procedure. The collector, whom he did not name, was Munro; his charge, the Ceded Districts.

Rickards' speech, which concluded with an argument for throwing open the Indian trade, roused Charles Grant and Henry Thornton to the defence of the Cornwallis system, of its 'wise, humane, and liberal principles', of the 'numerous precautions . . . taken to secure the just and equitable treatment of the . . . ryots'.[1] Grant—who had left India early in 1790—suggested that Rickards had not spoken from local knowledge, but 'had only referred to records', particularly the *Fifth Report*, and had drawn from that source an inference 'entirely different from that which the whole of the Report taken together, clearly and professedly presented'—indeed that he had so selected his evidence as to 'favour assertions and conclusions directly at variance with the main scope' of the Report.[1] Clearly then, Grant could not accept Rickards' case that the social disorder and lawlessness was the result of poverty and misgovernment: with the unquestioning piety of his evangelical faith he attributed it to 'the depraved principles and hereditary manners of the people'.[2] Thornton added his praise to the system of administration, and assured the House 'that he had . . . looked into the documents' and found that they 'did not at all bear out the conclusions' of Rickards.[3] It is hard to avoid concluding that Grant and Thornton had either failed to read the *Fifth Report*—in spite of Grant's membership of the committee responsible for it—or else that they were either wilfully or unconsciously attempting to mislead the House; for Lord Grenville, who was as unqualified as they were in his praise and support for the Cornwallis system, had read the report with 'deep concern and alarm'.[4] In defending the privileges of the Company they may have decided that it would be a tactical mistake to admit anything to be wrong with any aspect of the Company's activities. Rickards certainly deserves the last word, and was probably near the truth when he told the House that 'Justice, moderation, peace, and security, are ever proclaimed to be the object of our government in India—and a general consciousness that such is really and honestly intended, leads many to believe, that such really has been its practical effects.'[5]

Before the special committee of the Court which was considering revenue and judicial affairs had reported, the Board wrote to the Court expressing a desire that a despatch to Madras should be prepared 'upon the subject of the system of Criminal Justice and Police . . . as well as the administration of civil justice'.[6] Following the Court's reply, which assured the Board of their anxiety to forward 'this business as expeditiously as its very great moment and difficulty will permit', but argued that more time was needed to complete investigations of the subject,[7] the Board sent a strong letter repeating their request. In view of the information contained in the *Fifth Report*, in accounts both from the governments in India and from experienced servants of the Company, wrote the Board, they could not permit 'without modification or improvement the continuance of a system which, however excellent in principle, has not only in practice proved inadequate to the beneficient [*sic*] purposes of its author, but has had the effect in some degree of encreasing the evils which it was intended to remove'.[1] The report of the committee which, as we have already seen, was largely influenced by Munro's views, was approved by the Court on 9 March 1814,[2] and became the basis of a draft despatch to Fort St George[3] which was sent to the Board. It was returned by the Board, who had a draft of their own prepared. This would not, they wrote, 'in substance . . . be found to differ materially with respect to those points on which it treats from the opinions which have been expressed by the Court',[4] but in fact it went further than the Court's draft in its reforms.[5] It was accepted by the Court and became the Judicial Despatch to Madras of 29 April 1814.

The Court of Directors, in their draft despatch, advocated vesting the collection of the revenue, the administration of the police and criminal justice, and to a certain extent a share of judicial power, in one person. After quoting Munro's description of the village police and expressing doubt as to 'whether any system of police will ever be efficient in India which proceeds upon the basis of separating the office of magistrate from that of Collector', they directed that the control of the police should be transferred from the district judge to the collector, thus placing him 'on the same footing as the Provincial Amildar is said to have formerly been under the Native Governments'.[6] While being aware of the objections to uniting the two offices, the Court were inclined, they wrote, 'in some degree to accommodate [their] views to what [they] understood to be the manner and usages of the people of India, rather than to adhere to an abstract theory or even to approved practice in other countries'.[1] The magisterial powers to try petty cases, given the collectors by the Court, were extended by the Board; the extent of punishment by imprisonment which magistrates could impose, for example, being increased from fifteen days to three months, besides which they were empowered to inflict fines of up to ten pounds, a punishment 'not at all in the contemplation of the Court'.[2] For the administration of civil justice the Court remained convinced of the soundness of the system of district courts, but not of the ability of these courts to settle speedily petty causes; and for this purpose they judged it 'exceedingly desirable to revive the old institution of village courts and to give the Inhabitants an option of resorting to a Punchayet, or Native Jury for the settlement of their disputes'.[3] The powers given by the Court to the native commissioners and panchayats were increased by the Board. The final difference between the two drafts was that where the Court had given the Madras Government a discretionary power to postpone the execution of the instructions, if after consultation with the Sadr Adalat they should appear so exceptionable as to justify a further reference to the Court, in the Board's despatch this paragraph was omitted and the orders for the various changes were positive and final. In spite of these differences the Board of Control and the Court of Directors had finally come to agree on a plan of reform for the Madras judicial system, a plan almost exactly the same as that proposed by Munro in a memoir written just after his return from Madras, and four years before the *Fifth Report*.

The judicial code [he wrote] ought undoubtedly to be amended so as to return to the heads of villages their ancient jurisdiction in petty causes—to make all causes of importance be decided by Punchayets or Native Juries—to throw as much as possible of the administration of justice into the hands of intelligent natives instead of confining it to European Judges who can seldom be qualified to discharge the duty—and to reunite the office of magistrate to that of Collector.[4]

Agreement having thus been reached, Munro was sent back to Madras as Special Commissioner to revise the judicial system on the lines laid down by the despatch of 29 April. Nevertheless the relations between the two bodies were scarcely amicable. 'We are at open war with the Board—and the Court, Divided, Agitated beyond any thing I ever remember', Toone had written to Hastings a few months before.[1] The Board did not improve matters by sending 'peremptory and detailed instructions' to the governments in India 'on matters of Judicature, Police and Revenue, instructions tending to effect a great change in the system by which India has been administered for the last 20 years'; a course of proceeding which was believed by some of the Directors to have been 'not contemplated by the Legislature in the original institution of the Board'.[2] It is clear that the President and Board were interesting themselves in the administration of India to an extent that was unprecedented. The Board carried out its own investigation into ways of 'rendering the administration of Justice more expeditious and more efficient', as a preliminary to preparing their draft despatch to Madras and a later one to Bengal.[3] Thomas Courtenay, who was secretary to the Board from August 1812, later stated,

an inspection of the official drafts and letters of reasons gives a very imperfect idea indeed of the extent and of the nature of the superintendence and control exercised by the Board. In some departments, especially in the revenue and judicial department, that control was exercised in Lord Buckinghamshire's time; and subsequently, to a very great extent indeed, in matters involving great principles as well as in matters of detail. A very great proportion of the proceedings of the Board on this occasion was unofficial. I may here mention that the system known by the name of Sir Thomas Munro's system, was the work of the Board, and in many parts of it was opposed by the Court.[4]

It was not only in revenue and judicial questions that Buckinghamshire sought to extend the Board's control. The failure to follow the usual course of discussing a 'previous communication' when preparing a despatch, which apparently occurred with the judicial despatch to Madras of 29 April 1814. had also happened in July 1813, following the renewal of the Charter, with the despatch explaining the provisions of the new act to the governments in India. Buckinghamshire imposed a draft on the Court in which he 'alleged that the recent Act had established the complete predominance of the Board over the Court',[1] an assertion which the Directors denied. Thereafter almost every question that was discussed led to controversy between the Board and the Court, and Buckinghamshire, if not provoking the dispute by his impetuosity, generally aggravated the irritation by his tactlessness and apparent desire to humiliate the Directors. Only when Canning succeeded Buckinghamshire in June 1816 was there a reconciliation between the two bodies, one of the first results of which was a private conference between Canning and the 'Chairs', at which agreement was reached on the principles on which the home government's future policy on administration was to be based.

It has been written that in the period under review 'the home government [of India] had shown remarkable insight, wisdom and persistence in preventing the extension of the Bengal system to the Company's other territories'.[2] While there is some truth in this it is at the same time misleading. There was fortunate coincidence: the setting up of the parliamentary committee, Munro's trip home, Cumming's emergence from his clerk's obscurity. There is little to suggest that the organisation of the home government fitted it to be particularly sensitive to the need for a new policy, or that institutionally it was well equipped for grappling with such problems. Nevertheless a system of administration, paternal, authoritarian, based on the rule of the executive officer rather than the rule of law, was established and was to be lasting. Some of the ideas incorporated in it were to contribute to all subsequent British colonial administrative policy.

CHAPTER 5

MUNRO AS SPECIAL COMMISSIONER
1814-18

Appointed Special Commissioner for the revision of the Madras judicial system,[1] Munro arrived at Fort St George on 16 September 1814, and began at once to examine all the reports from the judges, collectors and commercial residents to the Committees of Police from 1805 to 1814. Of the recommendations of those committees, and of those contained in the Court's despatch of 29 April 1814, he found none had yet been carried into effect,[2] and it soon became quite clear that there was little enthusiasm at Fort St George for any administrative change.[3] Hugh Elliot,[4] the Governor, who had arrived at the same time as Munro, had been given the impression that 'everything was in the best possible state', that those reforms proposed by the Court which were practicable had in fact been anticipated, and that conditions had changed so much since Munro left India that he must abandon his former opinions.[5] 'You are aware', Munro wrote to Cumming, 'that most of the men in office about the Presidency are Regulation-men, stickling for every part of the present system, and opposers of every reform of it from home.'[6] Most of the men in office about the Presidency also failed to see why the reforms could not be left to the local government, or, if a special commissioner had to be appointed, why he should not have been chosen from among their number.[7] Eventually Munro's opponents resigned themselves to the fact that it was their 'business to keep the system going, to make no alterations, and leave all to the decision of the authorities in Europe';[8] but their success in delaying reforms clearly ordered by the Court must be considered in judging the effectiveness of the home government as an administrative body.

Munro's instructions were to carry out the reforms recommended in the Court's despatch of 29 April 1814.[1] Of these reforms 'by far the most important', in Munro's view, was the transfer of police and magisterial duties from the zillah judge to the collector: 'all the rest are subordinate to and dependent upon this, it must necessarily be carried into effect before any one of them can be brought forward.'[2] He therefore proposed that a short regulation should be prepared, free from all details, simply authorising the transfer, and leaving the collector, as magistrate, to be guided by the existing regulations until more comprehensive changes could be made. This the Council would not accept. They failed to agree with Munro's interpretation of the Court's despatch, finding orders for transferring to the collector only the super-intendence and control of the police, not the whole duties of magistrate; and in their view the modifications which the Court prescribed for the established system of judicature were not dependent on that transfer.[3] In the Council there was certainly strong opposition to giving the magistrate's power to the collector, thus uniting executive and judicial power in opposition to the whole basis of the Cornwallis tradition. 'If the Collector be vested with the power of punishment...' wrote Fullerton, 'there is reason to fear its misapplication to facilitate the ends of his executive duty— the deprivation of all such means of abuse may be considered a fixed principle from which it is safest not to depart; abstract principles may indeed in some cases be deviated from even with some practical advantage, but we must not lose sight of them.'[4] The Commission therefore—on which Munro had been joined by George Stratton,[5] who at the same time was appointed third member of the court of Sadr Adalat[6]—were required to confine themselves to the lesser transfer of power, but also to submit their opinion 'as to the expediency of the further transfer which Colonel Munro conceives to have been in the contemplation of the Court of Directors', and the opinions of the Sadr Adalat and the Board of Revenue on this question were also sought.[7]

Munro's immediate reaction was to write to Cumming, 'I think it necessary to caution you, that if it is expected that instructions are to be obeyed, the strongest and plainest words must be used. . . . unless the words "We direct,"—"We order," are employed, the measures to which they relate will be regarded as optional.'[1] To the Madras government the Commissioners reiterated the general case for transferring the office of magistrate entirely to the collector, and argued that throughout the Court's despatch of 29 April 1814 the chief objects had been

> that the collision of authorities should be prevented, the administration of justice be facilitated, and the expense of the Judicial establishment be diminished; but none of these can be accomplished, while the zillah Judge retains the office of magistrate, for the clashing of authorities must continue as before, by the village and district servants still remaining subject to the orders both of the Judge and the Collector, the administration of justice must still be impeded by a great portion of the Judge's time being occupied in magisterial duties, and no one court can be reduced in order to effect a saving, while the whole of the courts, by so much of the time of the Judges being so employed, are inadequate to the discharge of the business before them.[2]

This in effect was to refer the question back to the home government, and a reply to such a reference was unlikely to be received in much less than twelve months.

There was disagreement also over the procedure to be adopted in passing regulations to give effect to the other arrangements ordered by the Court of Directors. Munro proposed six regulations: the first to restore the management of the village police to the heads of villages, and of the district police to the tahsildars and amildars under the collector; the second for constituting heads of villages native commissioners and for directing village panchayats; the third for the appointment and guidance of native district judges or commissioners, and district panchayats; the fourth to authorise the collector as magistrate to enforce the patta regulations; the fifth to prevent zamindars and proprietors of land from distraining without the collector's authority; and the sixth a regulation placing the decision of cases of disputed boundaries in the hands of the collector.[1] If these were prepared and published with as little delay as possible, and circulated to the districts, the people would be shown the whole extent of the proposed changes and the Commission would be enabled to convince them that the modifications introduced were not intended to weaken or destroy the existing system, but to strengthen and improve it, bringing its advantages nearer to them. The Council, however, while directing the Commission to prepare such regulations, directed also that before they prepared them they should ascertain the number of the village officers to be employed under those regulations, their allowances in land, grain and money, and their willingness and competence to undertake the duties assigned to them; a course of proceeding which, Munro believed, would protract the business of the Commission 'far beyond the period limited by the Court of Directors'.[2] 'Who is to decide the point of [the patels'] competency', Munro wrote to Cumming, 'if it is not admitted to have been established by universal practice? for there is not a man about Government, and scarcely ten men in the provinces, who know the difference between a potail and a weaver.'[3]

The next difficulty arose from the discovery of a direction from Wellesley, as Governor-General in Council, to the Governor in Council at Fort St George, that all regulations proposed to be adopted for the internal government of the territories under Fort St George should be transmitted to the Governor-General in Council for his sanction previous to their final adoption. To Elliot it appeared that this could scarcely be meant to apply to regulations drawn up in conformity to orders issued by the Court of Directors; but under pressure from his Council he agreed at least to consult the supreme government on the question, while pointing out the delay which would thereby be caused.[4]

Almost one year after Munro's arrival back in India, he wrote to Cumming a gloomy account of the Commission's progress.

Why should we amuse ourselves with interchanges of sentiments, on things which have undergone a ten years' discussion, and which the Government at home had directed to be adopted? or of what use can it be, to import sentiments from Bengal, on punchayets and potails, which most of the public servants under that Presidency profess never to have heard of? I see no way of enabling the Commission to answer any of the objects of its institution, but by sending orders without delay to the Government here, to carry into immediate execution, without reference to, or waiting for an answer from Bengal to any reference that may have been made, all those modifications on which the Government at home have already made up their mind.

The proposed changes have many opponents; because there are only a few collectors who understand the nature of them, from not having seen potails and punchayets employed, before the introduction of the judicial code; they are opposed by many in the judicial line, who consider the present system, whatever it may be, as the best. They are opposed by some, from a sincere conviction that native agency is dangerous; and by some, because they have had no share in suggesting them; but the best founded motive of opposition is one which has only lately appeared, namely, the probability that the natives will give so much preference to the settlement of laws by heads of villages and punchayets, as to leave so little business to the zillah courts that many of them will be reduced. . . . In the outset, we shall have complaints from the judges of the ignorance of the potails and punchayets, their partiality and corruption. This will often be true; but the evil will be greatly overbalanced by the good.[1]

On receiving from Fort St George the papers showing the differences between the Judicial Commission and the government, the Court of Directors made their reply succinct and quite explicit. The transfer of the magistrate's duties to the collector had been intended by them, and this was in their opinion 'fairly deducible' from their despatch; and certainly it is difficult to see how the officials at Fort St George, had they been disinterested, could have come to any other conclusion. The Court could not agree that it was 'by no means necessary to the efficiency of the Collector's superintendence of police, that he should be invested with the powers of a magistrate'; they feared that the investigations asked for would prevent the early passing of the regulations concerning village courts and village police, and pronounced that the course suggested by the commission, of passing general regulations without delay and adjusting details subsequently was much to be preferred. The commissioners' arguments were so much in accord with the Court's, indeed, and had 'with so much accuracy and ability, defined the course which, in their opinion, ought to be pursued for the purpose of giving early effect to our instructions, that we cannot too strongly express our satisfaction at the additional evidence . . . of their peculiar fitness for the discharge of the important trust that has been committed to them.' The government at Fort St George, therefore, was directed to adopt the course urged by the commissioners. Finally Elliot's opinion was confirmed that regulations drawn up for the internal administration of Madras in conformity with orders of the home authorities need not be submitted to the Governor-General in Council for his sanction.[1]

The Court's despatch did not arrive at Fort St George until May 1816. In the meantime, the voluminous correspondence between the commission and the government was kept up, and Munro believed he found support for his arguments under conditions in Coimbatore. The great fault in the existing judicial system was that it established a series of courts and a judicial code which for a variety of reasons failed to protect the ryots, particularly in comparatively minor cases of oppression.

In order to protect rayets [Munro wrote to Cumming] it is not enough to wait for their complaints, we must go round and seek for them. . . . A renter who has four or five hundred rayets under him, imposes an extra assessment of ten or twelve per cent., and collects it, without difficulty or opposition, in the course of a few days. Suppose they should complain afterwards, which is seldom the case, the process of the court would occupy many months, probably some years, and they would be obliged to abandon their suit, from not being able, from their poverty, to wait its issue. . . . It will require a long course of years, perhaps ages, before they acquire sufficient courage and independence to resist; and until this change is effected, our present courts cannot protect them. We must adapt our institutions to their character; they can be protected only by giving to the collector authority to investigate extra collections, and to cause them to be refunded.[2]

There were reports of widespread corruption in the revenue affairs of Coimbatore. The Board of Revenue, with the exception of Cochrane (who had served under Munro in the Ceded Districts), refused to believe them.[1] Elliot, in spite of objections from the Board, on 26 September 1815 appointed Munro, together with John Sullivan,[2] the collector, to examine generally into the condition of the district.[3] Their report (dated 26 February 1816)[4] disclosed 'a scene of malversation, fraud and embezzlement' which, the Court of Directors trusted, stood 'unparalleled in the annals of British India'.[5] The Indian treasurer of the district had gradually obtained great ascendancy; he had been, in fact, the manager of the whole district, using native servants to carry on an extensive trade, and for several years levying extra revenue collections on twenty-five or thirty thousand of the inhabitants. Few of the inhabitants—'probably not twenty'—had ever sought redress from the courts, though Sullivan, on succeeding William Garrow as collector in 1815, in a few months received thousands of complaints; which led Munro and Sullivan to comment that it was 'impossible to resist the conclusion, that our institutions are inefficient'. The only effectual remedies they saw were to increase the pay of the higher classes of native revenue servants, and to empower the collector to investigate and determine all cases of extra collections and embezzlement and to recover the amount by summary process.

As Munro no doubt intended, the report proved 'a tender subject for most of the great authorities here, who did not believe there could be any abuses, where the regulations were so well understood',[6] and it was neither sent home nor referred to the Board of Revenue for over six months.[7] Though the critics of the judicial commission's proposals remained unconvinced by the corroboration thus lent to Munro's assertions, it is probable that the report was one explanation for the more effective support given the commission by Elliot, to whom it must have become quite clear that everything was certainly not in the 'best possible state' in the presidency. The arrival of the Court's despatch two months later would not lessen the impression.

In framing the regulations as instructed by the Council[1] Munro and Stratton endeavoured, they wrote, 'to adopt them as far as possible to the manners and institutions of the People for whose use they [were] intended',[2] and to that end they were made as simple as possible. But while the commissioners argued that all regulations 'should in the beginning conform as nearly as possible to the existing customs of the country', they added that institutions established on that basis ought not to be narrowly judged by their utility in settling causes, but rather by the beneficial effects on the character of the people which would follow from using Indians for administering justice.

Nothing surely [they wrote] can tend more strongly to raise men in their own estimation and to make them act up to it, than the being thought worthy of being entrusted with the distribution of Justice to their country men and no motives can be more powerful in attaching a body of men to a Government, than the consciousness that they are not neglected by it—that confidence is placed in them—and that though in a subordinate capacity, they form a material part of its internal administration.[3]

The draft regulations were sent to the Sadr Adalat for revision on 3 July 1815, and on 13 October Elliot recorded a minute directing the court to submit them immediately to government, or to state the cause of delay.[4] The court maintained that they had been as quick as possible, considering their other duties, and added that as the third judge, Stratton, was a member of the commission the revision had been carried out by the other members of the court.[5] This suggested that the Governor's intention, when he appointed Stratton a member both of the commission and of the court, to facilitate the work of reform had not been realised—a suggestion confirmed when the court's comments on the regulations were finally laid before the Governor in Council.[6]

Not merely did the court seek to show 'wherein the principle of the proposed enactments appears to be objectionable'. In spite of disclaiming a more detailed purpose, it entered into a lengthy consideration and criticism of the wording of the proposed regulations—matters which, had there been cooperation between Stratton's colleagues and himself, could in the main have been settled by word of mouth, and correspondence, if necessary, thus confined to points of substance. The court submitted its own redrafted regulations, and on 1 March 1816—eight months after the commission's drafts had been sent to the court—these were transmitted to Munro and Stratton. Their conclusion was that

most of the difficulties seen by the Sudder Adawlut originate in their viewing the Potail, not as what he is, a head Ryot engaged in agriculture and deciding one or two petty suits in the year, but as a regular Judge, solely occupied in hearing causes from one end of the year to the other. They speak of his sitting in open court, of the respectability of the judicial character, of preserving the purity of these inferior judicatories, of his conscience not being bound by an oath, of his being subject to no controul, and of the ease with which he may convert his power into an engine of oppression. We are satisfied that the evil or the good that any one village Moonsiff can do will be trifling; that oppression will seldom be within the power of any one of them, and is sufficiently open to punishment; that good will be within the reach of them all, and that however little may be done by them individually, the aggregate will be great.[1]

Even Fullerton saw that those arguments of the Sadr Adalat relating to the general incompatibility of the offices of patel and village judge, while perhaps unanswerable if certain general principles were assumed, were irrelevant when the avowed policy was to deviate from those principles

in search of a practical good. Our object [he wrote] is to administer speedy and summary justice on petty disputes to the lower order of the people, without expense to them, and without additional charge to Government. The selection of heads of villages as Judges is the only one within our reach, without additional expense, and the dispensation with form, as far as possible, affords the only means of bringing into operation the speedy administration of justice.[2]

And as Munro wrote to Cumming, 'the great advantages of the village regulations are, that they do not touch the existing judicial system, but leave it to go on as before.' Should the inhabitants prefer to use the regular courts established under the old code rather than the patels and panchayats they would be able to do so.

Only experience could show which system was best suited to the needs of the inhabitants.[1]

The commission's final draft of the regulations was submitted to the Council by Elliot on 25 April 1816.[2] There were seven of them. The first declared the head inhabitants of villages to be munsiffs in their respective villages, hearing and deciding civil suits to a limited amount. The second authorised them to assemble village panchayats, and defined the power and authority to be vested in these. This would restore to the patels, Munro believed, the authority in the village which they had formerly possessed, but had lost through the introduction of the judicial regulations— except where they had been appointed to act as commissioners under the judge. Trial by panchayat he held to have been the most common way of deciding suits under the native governments; and, the commission being satisfied that the general form of panchayat assembled by the Indians would 'under proper control answer all the purposes for which it [was] intended',[3] the regulation largely followed the custom of the country. It prescribed, for instance, that the panchayat should be composed partly of persons of the same caste as the respective parties, and partly of persons of a caste different from that of both. In number, however, it was to be limited to eleven, as a greater number (so ran the argument), although by no means uncommon especially in litigation over village land, would serve only to create confusion and delay.

The third regulation defined the powers of the district munsiffs, and the fourth authorised them to assemble district panchayats. Men well qualified for the position of district munsiff, the commission believed, might be found among the servants of the zillah courts, and the promotion of such of them as were deserving would be a 'judicious mode of rewarding and encouraging others to a zealous discharge of their duty'.[4] The district munsiffs were empowered to refer to a district panchayat suits for real or personal property to a limited value; thus again following the 'principle of employing the better informed of the inhabitants generally in the administration of Justice'.[1] The fifth regulation provided for the appointment of the Indian law officers of the provincial courts to be head native commissioners and to hear cases referred to them by the zillah judges.[2] The sixth covered the settlement of disputes over village boundaries: the collector being empowered to assemble a panchayat through the district munsiff, the decision of which he must either confirm or annul if it should be proved to show gross partiality or corruption, but otherwise he had no power to interfere in the proceedings.

By the seventh regulation the superintendence of the police was transferred from the zillah magistrate to the collector, the daroga establishment was abolished and the police of villages placed under the immediate direction of the patels, of districts under that of tahsildars, and of provinces, under the collector. Here, again, the primary purpose of the regulation was to revive the traditional practice; to base the police on the village servants who had formerly had those duties, making the position hereditary, and partly remunerated by inam, rather than trying to build up a separate organisation with no special links with particular villages, and without the knowledge which the village police gained through being employed also as part of the revenue establishment.

The passing of the regulations was opposed by both Fullerton and Robert Alexander, president of the Board of Revenue and a member of the Council,[3] who once more proposed referring them to the supreme government.[4] Their objections rested on two main grounds: that the information on the village officers which the Council had directed the commission to collect had not been provided; and, secondly, that the commission's munsiff regulation, which allowed for the employment in that position of village renters where such existed, in place of hereditary patels, was 'repugnant to the principles laid down by the orders of the Court'.[5] It appeared essential to Alexander that 'the head inhabitants . . . should be maintained in their stations; which, for the duties expected from them to be successfully executed, should be

confirmed, and independent either of any renter or renter's agent
... the renter does not rent the rights of the Potail but those of the
Sircar, which are entirely distinct and independent.'[1] This was a
difficulty which could not arise with a ryotwari settlement which
would ensure the service of the patel as munsiff. Fullerton's and
Alexander's objections and suggested alterations were discussed
with the commissioners by Elliot, and after certain amendments
had been adopted, the regulations were passed and sent to the press
for printing.[2]

Within the next fortnight the Court's despatch of 20 December
1815, giving unqualified support to the proposals and course of
proceeding originally suggested by Munro and Stratton, arrived
at Fort St George. The printing of the police and boundary
regulations was suspended, and the commission directed to
prepare three new regulations: the first modifying and defining the
power of magistrate and transferring the office from the zillah
judge to the collector; the second consequently redefining the
power of the zillah judge; and the third establishing a general
system of police under the collector as magistrate.[3] The commission's drafts were laid before the Council on 8 July 1816,[4] and sent
to the Sadr Adalat, which was required, in revising them, to
'abstain from all discussion with regard to the principles laid down
in the letter from the Court of Directors ... and as it is considered
of great importance to avoid delay' their report was to be submitted within fifteen days of receipt of the drafts.[5] The court
failed to make any revision of the regulations, claiming that there
was too little time, so that the commissioners revised and corrected
them themselves.[6] The court did, however, record at some length
proceedings which suggested that a 'preferable arrangement to
that proposed by the Commission [would be] to constitute the
Collector Police Magistrate, and to leave to the Judge the office of
Zillah Magistrate', a plan so much at variance with the Court of
Directors' intentions, that the commissioners saw no reason to
wait for its details, but rather recommended that their drafts be

passed without further delay.[1] This advice was accepted by Elliot, and the three regulations were passed on 13 September 1816.[2] A fourth regulation, providing that disputes over the occupying, cultivating and irrigating of land as well as boundary disputes should be determined by the collector upon the verdict of a panchayat, was passed at the same time.[3]

Fullerton and Alexander recorded objections,[4] and while Fullerton admitted that his views on the transfer of magisterial power to the collector had proved to be at variance with those of the Court of Directors, he could not resist once more invoking the principle of 'the due separation of executive and judicial duties', which 'since the establishment of a regular system of government, [had] been deemed indispensable'. It is little wonder that Munro wrote to Cumming,

it is only a waste of time to continue the discussion about the new arrangements. The only way is to let them have a fair trial, like their predecessors, for eight or ten years' experience will show which is best; the natives will decide the question. If they settle their disputes among themselves, through heads of villages and punchayets, and leave the courts with not half their present business, it will be pretty evident that they have got something they like better.[5]

Elliot himself wrote the next day to W. F. Elphinstone in terms so similar as to leave little doubt that he had been convinced by Munro's arguments: 'the new Judicial System must in some degree be considered as an experiment called for by the defects of the former system, which in its turn will no doubt be subject to improvement or correction. I have endeavoured to ascertain what was the true import of the instructions sent out by the Court of Directors, and in as much as I thought the regulations proposed by the commissioners to be conformable to those instructions, I have given them my hearty and finally effective support.'[6]

The regulations having been completed and promulgated, Munro decided to visit various districts to observe the progress made in introducing the new system, and to investigate any difficulties that might arise. He was authorised, as well, to make such enquiries into the revenue affairs of the districts through which he was to pass as he might think useful, and to report his observations to government.[1] After being delayed at Fort St George by illness, he finally left for Tanjore early in 1817. He found there that out of 6,011 villages, patels had been appointed in 4,108; and of the 1,903 without patels, Munro estimated that about 600 were uninhabited, leaving 1,303. Of these 140 belonged to the raja, and a large proportion of the remainder were rented, so that Munro concluded that very few, if any, would be left for which patels might not be provided under the regulations. It appeared, however, that many patels appointed had refused to act, and when Munro, at a meeting with the principal landholders of the Myaveram district, pointed out that their duties under the new regulations in no essential way differed from those to which they had always been accustomed, they simply objected that their time was so much occupied in cultivation and finding the means of paying their rents that they had none to spare for other duties. They objected also that in a mirasi village no mirasdar had authority superior to another; but Munro found strong evidence against this, that in villages held by a number of mirasdars there was one with the title of natumkar who exercised authority over the rest, and was as capable as the head ryots of other districts of acting as the head of the village. Having met this opposition Munro argued, not without a touch of disingenuousness, that to hear the opinions of the large number of individuals concerned as to their being willing or not willing to undertake the office of patel 'answers no purpose but to raise difficulties and occasion delay', and suggested that such opinions were generally influenced by a few leading men in each district. But the main cause of the delay in establishing the patels in Tanjore was not connected with the particular institutions of that district; in Munro's opinion they 'had arisen from the Collector not having taken the steps calculated to ensure success to the measure'.[2]

From Tanjore Munro went to Trichinopoly, Madura, Dindigul

and Coimbatore, in all of which he found the same general system of village affairs being directed by a head cultivator. He believed, however, that the efficiency of the village system had been considerably diminished under the Company's government. By constant removals the patel's office in some districts had been rendered more a temporary appointment than an inheritance, and in other ways its rights had often been whittled down. In spite of this the heads of villages were capable of carrying on all the duties required of them by the new regulations, although they would do it better, in Munro's opinion, if the situations were rendered more fixed and independent, which would give the patels more weight and respectability in the country. In these provinces Munro found that the changes brought in by the new regulations had produced general satisfaction.[1]

In Malabar Munro's investigations satisfied him that the village establishment was so inadequate to the object of its institution that it required a complete revision. Under the Malabar rajas the system had been adapted to the ends of military government; after Haidar's invasion there was never time or tranquillity to complete a new one, and the villages were run almost entirely by the district establishment under the tahsildar. Under the British the system had not greatly altered; it depended on poorly paid Indian district servants, there were no means of obtaining and preserving detailed village accounts, and the gap between the collector and the landholders was so great as to place everything respecting their real condition out of his sight. The position, in Munro's view, was such as to jeopardise the Company's security.

Our Government [he wrote] rests almost entirely upon the single point of military power: there is no native one which rests so exclusively upon it. Where there is no village establishment, we have no hold upon the people, no means of acting upon them, none of establishing confidence. Our situation, as foreigners, renders a regular village establishment more important to us than to a native Government: our inexperience, and our ignorance of the circumstances of the people, make it more necessary for us to seek the aid of regular establishments to direct the internal affairs of the country, and our security requires that we should have a body of head men of villages interested in supporting our dominion.

This reasoning being probably more applicable to Malabar than to any other province, Munro proposed that a regular village establishment should be introduced, and that the district servants should be rendered more respectable by increased allowances.[1]

How far the results of Munro's enquiries on his tour bore out his contention that the best way of proceeding was to pass general regulations, and subsequently add to them if experience showed this to be necessary, was by no means a matter of agreement at the time. Fullerton, who admitted that in most of the territories under Fort St George the plan 'had succeeded and [was] going on well', certainly still thought that 'instead of founding a law on presumption of a general state of things, not everywhere existing ... a preparatory systematick arrangement [should have been] made to place things exactly in the state contemplated by the Court of Directors'.[2] This scarcely seems a practicable alternative, if it is accepted that the condition of the unreformed judicial system was so inefficient as to call for rapid alteration. It is clear that Munro had not founded the regulations on a presumption of a general state of things; he was aware of local variations in village and district institutions. His tour did suggest, however, that except in the case of Malabar, these variations did not present great problems on putting the regulations into effect, and it is difficult to see that anything would have been gained if the regulations had been held in abeyance until a regular village establishment had been introduced into Malabar.

The government decided that the commission should cease on 3 January 1818, that being three years from the date of its complete formation, and on 19 August 1817 called for a report giving a general view of the new system actually in operation.[3] In July, however, Munro had accepted the command of a force ordered to take possession of Dharwar, which the Peshwa had ceded to the British government by the treaty of Poona. After spending some weeks at Dharwar, arranging with Maratha commissioners the limits of the districts which had been ceded, Munro learnt on 14 November that the Peshwa had begun hostilities by attacking the Poona residency, and for the next ten months Munro was actively engaged as a soldier in the Maratha war. He was promoted from Colonel to Brigadier-General in December 1817, and with an inadequate force, mainly of irregular soldiers, waged a brilliant campaign, reducing all the Peshwa's territory between the Tungabhadra and Krishna rivers. John Malcolm wrote of it with his customary enthusiasm:

Insulated in an enemy's country, with no military means whatever, (five disposable companies of sepoys were nothing,) he forms the plan of subduing the country, expelling the army by which it is occupied, and collecting the revenues that are due to the enemy, through the means of the inhabitants themselves, aided and supported by a few irregular infantry, whom he invites from the neighbouring provinces for that purpose. His plan, which is at once simple and great, is successful in a degree, that a mind like his could alone have anticipated.[1]

When the date for the judicial commission's ending arrived there was no immediate prospect of Munro's return to Madras, and it was decided that while Stratton's appointment should be continued until the end of March, the allowances to Munro as First Commissioner must cease, as he was fully occupied on military duties.[2] On 8 August he resigned his command, after experiencing considerable trouble with his eyes, and returned to the presidency intending to leave for Britain. It was not, however, until 24 January 1819 that he and his wife sailed in the *Warren Hastings*.

On Munro's return to Madras, Elliot had expressed a desire to re-establish the commission to finish what he thought was still incomplete in its business. To this Munro could not agree, for 'having relinquished a military command merely on account of the state of [his] eyes, it was impossible that [he] could accept a civil situation which from the very nature of its duties must prove much more injurious to them.'[3] He and Stratton did, however, write a final report surveying the extent to which the regulations were in practical operation.[1] While they cautiously asserted that some years must elapse before any correct judgment could be formed on the effect of the regulations, the figures available did suggest that in the field of civil justice their intention had been strikingly achieved. The number of suits settled by native courts had greatly increased; in 1817, the first year of operation of the new system, the total number of causes settled was nearly double that of any year of the old one.[2] Some of this number were settled in the very villages in which the suits arose, saving the inhabitants both time and money by being decided more expeditiously and nearer home, and by some of them again being exempted from all fees and charges. In criminal cases they believed the operation of the system to have been 'too short to furnish any sure grounds for estimating its effects'; nor could any sudden change in the state of crime be expected, because this depended not so much on the provisions for apprehending the criminals, as on 'the state of society, of the country, of peace or war, of plenty or scarcity'.[3]

For Munro, the work of the commission had been directed to one main end, that of employing Indians more extensively in the internal administration of the country. In every department, whatever could best be done by native servants should, he believed, be entrusted to them. 'The business of the European officer should principally be to control and direct properly the labours of the natives under him.'[4] In the discharge of all subordinate duties, especially judicial ones, Indians not only cost less, but being 'infinitely better qualified', were more efficient than Europeans. To the objection that they were too corrupt to be trusted, Munro replied that the Company's European servants had been notoriously corrupt until Cornwallis purchased their integrity by raising their allowances. The same thing could be done for the Indian servants. From the arguments of efficiency and economy Munro went further, to the very basis of British power in India, to question the wisdom of the prevailing British view of the Company's Indian subjects.

Our Government [he wrote to Hastings] will always be respected from the influence of our Military Power but it will never be popular while it offers no Employment to the Natives that can stimulate the ambition of the better classes of them. Foreign conquerors have treated the Natives with violence and often with great cruelty, but none has treated them with so much scorn as we have done. None has stigmatised a whole people as unworthy of trust, as incapable of honesty and as fit to be employed only when we cannot do without them. It seems to me not only ungenerous but impolitic to debase the character of a people fallen under our dominion. And nothing can more certainly produce this effect than our avowing our want of confidence in them and on that account excluding them as much as possible from every office of importance.[1]

CONCLUSION

Munro succeeded Elliot as governor of Madras on 10 June 1820, and was to remain in office until his death on 6 July 1827. His governorship was not marked by great changes or far-reaching new reforms: his main tasks, he considered, were rather to be the full application of the judicial reforms carried by the Special Commission in 1816, and the establishment of an effective ryotwari system in those districts where the decennial village leases were coming to an end. In his minutes, however, and above all in that of 31 December 1824, 'On the state of the Country, and the condition of the people', Munro, drawing upon the experience of the previous thirty years, gave clear expression to those views on administration which had developed since his first appointment to the Baramahal in 1792.[1]

There were no illusions in his mind as to the British position in India: 'the tenure by which we hold our power never has been, and never can be, the liberties of the people';[2] but having achieved that power, there were two important points which he believed should always be kept in view. The first was that British sovereignty 'should always be prolonged to the remotest possible period'; the second, that whenever they should be obliged to resign that power, they 'should leave the natives so far improved from their connection with [the British], as to be capable of maintaining a free, or at least a regular government amongst themselves'.[3]

We should look upon India [he wrote] not as a temporary possession, but as one which is to be maintained permanently, until the natives shall in some future age have abandoned most of their superstitions and prejudices, and become sufficiently enlightened to frame a regular Government for themselves, and to conduct and preserve it. Whenever such a time shall arrive, it will probably be best for both countries that the British control over India should be gradually withdrawn. That the desirable change here contemplated may in some after-age be effected in India, there is no cause to despair. Such a change was at one time in Britain itself, at least as hopeless as it is here. When we reflect how much the character of nations has always been influenced by that of Governments, and that some, once the most cultivated, have sunk into barbarism, while others, formerly the rudest, have attained the highest point of civilization, we shall see no reason to doubt, that if we pursue steadily the proper measures, we shall in time so far improve the character of our Indian subjects, as to enable them to govern and protect themselves.[1]

There is little to indicate how long a period Munro believed would be necessary for this change, if indeed he ever considered the question. Writing to Elphinstone, with the news that he had increased the number of Indians employed by the Board of Revenue at Madras, he pointed out the advantage of opening a field to 'able and aspiring Natives', and preparing the way 'for giving them some share in the Government half a century or a whole century hence'.[2] If he was uncertain about the timing, he held firmly that the principle that the Indians should be prepared to govern the country at some future date must be clearly established as the basic aim of British policy.

The chief danger to the continuance of British sovereignty lay in the spreading of disaffection in the native army.

In countries not under a foreign government, the spirit of freedom usually grows up with the gradual progress of early education and knowledge among the body of the people. This is its natural origin; and were it to rise in this way in this country while under our rule, its course would be quiet and uniform, unattended by any sudden commotion, and the change in the character and opinions of the people might be met by suitable changes in the form of government. But we cannot with any reason expect this silent and tranquil renovation; for, owing to the unnatural situation in which India will be placed under a foreign government with a free press and a native army, the spirit of independence will spring up in this army long before it is ever thought of among the people. The army will not wait for the slow operation of the instruction of the people, and the growth of liberty among them, but will hasten to execute their own measures for the overthrow of the Government.[3]

Should such a situation come about, the British, Munro believed, could not expect any aid from the people. The native army would be joined by all who had lost office through the British assumption of power, and by those who believed they could do better if the country reverted to its old rulers. 'We delude ourselves', Munro wrote, 'if we believe that gratitude for the protection they have received, or attachment to our mild Government, would induce any considerable body of the people to side with us in a struggle with the native army'.[1] Munro considerably overestimated the part the press could play in stirring up the troops,[2] but his accuracy in drawing attention to the native army as the key to British security was proved sound just over thirty years later.

While Munro was far from sharing the evangelical's horror or the utilitarian's scorn for Indian society, he did believe that in the 'knowledge of the theory and practice of good government' the Indians were 'much inferior to Europeans',[3] and whatever steps were taken to improve them in this capacity, it would be very long before any change was effected.[4] He emphasised that the problem was basically not social, or educational, or religious, but political.

We profess to seek [the Indians'] improvement [he wrote], but propose means the most adverse to success. The advocates of improvement do not seem to have perceived the great springs on which it depends; they propose to place no confidence in the natives, to give them no authority, and to exclude them from office as much as possible; but they are ardent in their zeal for enlightening them by the general diffusion of knowledge. . . . Our books alone will do little or nothing; dry simple literature will never improve the character of a nation. To produce this effect, it must open the road to wealth, and honour, and public employment. Without the prospect of such reward, no attainments in science will ever raise the character of a people.[5]

This view of Munro's was in marked contrast with that of the evangelicals, most clearly expressed by Charles Grant in his *Observations on the State of Society among the Asiatic Subjects of Great Britain.*[6] As a plea for the evangelisation of India, Grant's tract was in large part devoted to proving the necessity for this formidable task. The picture of Indian society which emerges from his writing would not have been recognised by Munro, who had testified before the House of Commons in 1813, that 'if civilization is to become an article of trade between [Britian and India], I am convinced that this country will gain by the import cargo'.[1] Grant, on the other hand, drew a picture of immeasurable super-stition and social corruption, of 'a race of men lamentably degenerate and base ... governed by malevolent and licentious passions, strongly exemplifying the effects produced on society by a great and general corruption of manners, and sunk in misery by their vices.'[2] The only cure for this evil was the redemption of the individual Indian soul, through its awakening to the truths of evangelical Christianity; and Grant argued that the mind could be freed of error and superstition, and prepared for Christian know-ledge, by education.[3] Education would pave the way for Christian-ity: if Christianity flourished, India would flourish in the material sense—and so would the British commercial interest. This view was strongly attacked by James Mill in his *History of British India*. With Munro, he held that the population of India suffered, not from lack of revealed Truth, but from poverty. 'The form of government is one', he wrote, 'the nature of the laws for the administration of justice is the other, of the two circumstances by which the condition of the people in all countries is chiefly deter-mined.'[4] To change India, something far beyond mere schooling was required:

The most efficient part of education is that which is derived from the tone and temper of society; and the tone and temper of society depend altogether upon the laws and the government. Again: ignorance is the natural concomitant of poverty; a people wretchedly poor are always ignorant; but poverty is the effect of bad laws, and bad government; and is never a characteristic of any people who are governed well. It is necessary, therefore, before education can operate to any great result, that the poverty of the people should be redressed; that their laws and government should operate beneficently.[5]

But while Mill and Munro agreed on the negligible part education alone could play in elevating the character and improv-ing the condition of the Indian population, their agreement stopped there. Mill rejected the idea that the employment of Indians in the higher branches of the administration would tend to elevate the character of the people as a whole.[1] The important thing was that government should be efficiently and cheaply run. In practice this led Mill to support various administrative methods also advocated by Munro, such as the ryotwari settlement, and the fusion to a large extent of executive and judicial powers. But the ways in which they arrived at these positions were entirely opposed in spirit. This is brought out clearly by Munro when he writes:

Even if we could suppose that it were practicable without the aid of a single native, to conduct the whole affairs of the country, both in the higher and in all the subordinate offices, by means of Europeans, it ought not to be done, because it would be both politically and morally wrong. The great number of public offices in which the natives are employed, is one of the strongest causes of their attachment to our Government. In proportion as we exclude them from these, we lose our hold upon them, and were the exclusion entire, we should have their hatred in place of their attachment. . . . But were it possible that they could submit silently and without opposition, the case would be worse; they would sink in character, they would lose with the hope of public office and distinction all laudable ambition, and would degenerate into an indolent and abject race, incapable of any higher pursuit than the mere gratification of their appetites. It would certainly be more desirable that we should be expelled from the country altogether, than that the result of our system of government should be such a debasement of a whole people. This is, to be sure, supposing an extreme case, because nobody has ever proposed to exclude the natives from the numerous petty offices, but only from the more important offices now filled by them. But the principle is the same, the difference is only in degree; for in proportion as we exclude them from the higher offices, and a share in the management of public affairs, we lessen their interest in the concerns of the community and degrade their character.[2]

Clearly then, it would be misleading to discuss 'the Munro system' purely in terms of forms of administration; certainly it would be doing less than justice to Munro himself. What marked Munro off from most of his successors, imbued as they were with evangelical ardour or Benthamite ruthlessness (or a combination of the two) was his understanding of the essential fact that if political advance did not keep pace with the general progress of government, nothing but bitterness and frustration could result.[1] If he was a paternalist, his was an extraordinarily sympathetic paternalism. The argument that only self-government can give a subject society the initiative and strength to bring about its economic and social regeneration may be the result of twentieth-century developments and ideas, but, in theory at least, Munro had grasped its truth. It was India's misfortune that his successors ignored this aspect of his 'system' completely.

Munro recognised, however, that in his time the preservation of British dominion in India required that all the higher offices, civil and military, should be filled by Europeans. Such officials, he always insisted, must be both well-informed and sympathetic. For its knowledge of the state of the country, government was entirely dependent upon its local officers: it made laws for a people with no voice in the matter, and could not adapt those laws to the condition of the people unless it received accurate information from active and intelligent officers, who had investigated carefully not only the condition but also the opinions of that people. Above all else these officers must know thoroughly the details of land tenure and revenue. 'Unless we know in what manner the land of a province is occupied', Munro wrote, 'we can form no just opinion as to how its internal administration should be regulated.'[2] The success of the administration depended directly on the efficiency of the collectors, 'by far the most important public functionaries of the Government';[3] but the revenue system, in Munro's view, had been neglected. 'It has unfortunately been regarded as a mere business of tax-gathering, and the Collectors as a set of Tax-Gatherers. Their denomination is a bad one, and has no doubt contributed to keep up this opinion both at home and in this country.'[4] The influence of the collector, in fact, extended to 'everything affecting the welfare of the people'.[5]

In India [he wrote] whoever regulates the assessment of the land rent holds in his hand the mainspring of the peace of the country, an equal and moderate assessment has more effect in preventing litigation and crimes than all our Civil and Criminal Regulations. When the lands are accurately surveyed and registered the numerous suits which occur where this is not the case regarding their boundaries and possession are prevented and when the assessment is moderate every man finds employment, and the thefts and robberies which are committed in consequence of the want of it and of other means of subsistence almost entirely cease. . . . If we have no correct detailed accounts of the lands, litigations will increase every day and all our courts will be inadequate to the adjustment of them. Nothing can so effectually lighten and diminish the business of the Courts as a good settlement of the Revenue.[1]

Munro advocated a gradation of revenue servants, in order both to ensure a supply of trained men to become collectors, and to provide positions for men of experience who previously, after some years as collectors, had almost invariably been drawn off into judicial appointments. A start should be made, he wrote, by getting principal collectors for the larger unsettled districts. When that had been done, men should be found capable of superintending the whole of a division, such as the Northern Circars. The principal collector would manage personally the whole of his district, excepting those portions placed under sub-collectors. The collector of a division would have no direct management, but would superintend the whole through the district collectors.[2] Only in such a way could they secure a succession of servants capable of conducting the internal administration of the country in an efficient manner, and achieve also the concentration of authority which Munro held to be vital. The best way of improving the efficiency of the civil service as a whole would be to make every civil servant begin his career in the revenue line. This would train an adequate number of men fit to become collectors; and, equally important, by giving the young European a thorough knowledge of the Indians it would, in Munro's view, give him a favourable view of them. By placing a sub-collector in a district of moderate extent, and relieving him from all correspondence except with the principal collector, he would be given ample time to become acquainted with the details of every branch of the revenue, and to acquire an intensive knowledge of village institutions. As Munro wrote to Elphinstone,

Almost everything that I know of Revenue details I learned as a Sub Coll. in the management of a territory of about fifty or sixty miles square yielding a Revenue of about 5 lacs of Rupees. It is the best of all Schools. As a Principal Collector I learned little—I had not time to pursue minute inquiries—I merely carried into practice what I had learned as a Sub.[1]

Experience, in his view, was the only real training for a collector; day to day work among the Indians was worth more than 'the study of all the Regulations and Codes of Calcutta and Madras together'.[2] An obsession with regulations was the peculiar fault of the judicial service, and a young man beginning his career there, finding himself all at once invested with judicial functions, learnt forms before he learnt things. 'He becomes full of respect due to the Court but knows nothing of the people. He is placed too high above them to have any general intercourse with them. He has little opportunity of seeing them except in Court. He sees only the worst part of them and under the worst shapes.'[3] Such a training could not qualify the Company's servants to govern India, for, Munro wrote, 'we can never be qualified to govern men against whom we are prejudiced. If we entertain a prejudice at all it ought rather to be in their favour than against them. We ought to know their character but especially the favourable side of it, for if we know only the unfavourable it will beget contempt and harshness on the one part and discontent on the other.'[4]

This insistence on the collector's keeping in the closest possible touch with the people under his care was one of the reasons leading to Munro's support for a ryotwari settlement. If a European was placed in charge of a district permanently settled, and in the hands of a few great zamindars who conducted all the details of the assessment and collection of the revenue, he had very little to do. No great knowledge was demanded from him, nor in fact was the best means of acquiring it open to him. Not only did this mean that the collector was poorly prepared to deal with any problems that arose which could not be left in the hands of the zamindars, but the permanence of the settlement ensured that such a situation was irrevocable.

> We proceed [Munro wrote] in a country of which we know little or nothing, as if we knew every thing, and as if every thing must be done now, and nothing could be done hereafter. We feel our ignorance of Indian revenue, and the difficulties arising from it; and instead of seeking to remedy it by acquiring more knowledge, we endeavour to get rid of the difficulty by precipitately making permanent settlements, which relieve us from the troublesome task of minute or accurate investigations, and which are better adapted to perpetuate our ignorance than to protect the people.[1]

The argument for a ryotwari settlement went much further than this. The haste with which the British had acted, Munro believed, and the way in which they had been 'led away by fanciful theories founded on European models', would inevitably lead to disappointment. By rushing in and declaring apparent rights to be permanent, they were running a risk of giving to one class what belonged to another. On the other hand, if they proceeded with patience, their knowledge of the manners and customs of the people and the nature and resources of the country would so increase as to enable them to 'frame gradually from the existing institutions' such a system as would advance the prosperity of the country, and be satisfactory to the people. 'The knowledge most necessary for this end', Munro wrote, 'is that of the landed property and its assessment, for the land is not only the great source of the public revenue, but on its fair and moderate assessment depend the comfort and happiness of the people.'[2] There was no doubt in Munro's mind that such knowledge would reveal some form of ryotwari settlement to be that most widely existing. The terms in which he saw the issue are clearly shown when he writes:

> The question is, whether we are to continue the country in its natural state, occupied by a great body of independent Rayets, and to enable them, by a lighter assessment, to rise gradually to the rank of landlords; or whether we are to place

129

the country in an artificial state, by dividing it in villages, or larger districts, among a new class of landholders, who will inevitably, at no distant period, by the subdivision of their new property, fall to the level of Rayets, while the Rayets will, at the same time, have sunk from the rank of independent tenants in chief, to that of sub-tenants and cultivators. . . . This question, it is to be hoped, has been set at rest by the orders of the Court of Directors, to make the settlement with the Rayets, in all districts in which the permanent Zamindarry settlement has not been established.[1]

Munro wanted the country to remain in its natural state, and to be occupied by a great body of independent ryots: two character-istics which we have seen that he believed to be complementary. He was then, in a definite sense, a conservative. But one cannot simply leave it at that. It is significant that the state which he advocated was the 'natural', rather than the 'established' or 'ancient', one. His argument took this form partly because, by the first years of the nineteenth century, the Bengal system was established as the orthodox pattern of British administration, and to many of the Company's servants Munro's opposition to this system marked him as an innovator rather than a conservative. But his argument is the result also of his conservatism being emotional as well as practical. The 'natural' state was one which, Munro believed, could be discovered through historical investiga-tion. In this sense the 'natural' state and the 'ancient' one were the same, provided one got back to the right stage of antiquity. This is at the very centre of Munro's thought, and marks him off clearly both from the Cornwallis school, and from his own utilitarian successors. Munro shared Burke's reverence for the past, for its accumulated wisdom, as well as being sceptical of the possibility of any great or lasting change in society being brought about by government action or legislation. Munro's Nature was that of Wordsworth and the Romantic movement. After a meeting with him, Elphinstone recorded that Munro had 'discovered an acquaintance with literature, a taste and relish for poetry, and an ardent and romantic turn of mind';[2] and later, that under 'his plain and somewhat stern demeanour', Munro concealed 'a delicacy of taste and tenderness of feeling'.[1] They were qualities that, indeed, Munro had possessed since youth. To his sister he wrote, in 1790:

I spend many of my leisure hours on the highest summit of the rock on which the fort stands, under the shady side of a bastion built by Hyder.

This spot has for me a certain charm, which I always strongly feel, but cannot easily describe. . . . While seated on the rock, I am, or fancy that I am, more thoughtful than when below. The extent and grandeur of the scene raises my mind, and the solitude and silence make me think that 'I am conversing with Nature here'.

To the east, I see a romantic and well-cultivated valley, leading to the wide plains of the Carnatic. To the south, a continuation of the same valley, running as far as the eye can reach, into Mysore. All the rest, on every side, is a vast assemblage of hills and naked rocks, wildly heaped one above another.[2]

To the end of his life he was moved by 'wild and magnificent scenes of nature'.[3]

In his view, too, of the virtue of a simple peasant life, Munro was at one with the Romantics. To Colonel Read he described the pleasure which he had often felt in Kanara, and never experienced in any other part of India, 'in seeing myself at the time of the Jummabundy, under the fly of a tent, among some large trees, surrounded by four or five hundred landlords, all as independent in their circumstances as your yeomen'.[4] Such a society, he believed, needed the simplest of governments; instead of which, the Cornwallis system was imposing on it English institutions and English ideas. There were even, in Munro's view, some down-right Englishmen who would 'insist on making Anglo-Saxons of the Hindoos'.[5] For this conviction he found support in the government records.

I have never had a very high opinion of our records [he wrote to Canning]; but it was not until my last return that I knew that they contained such a mass of useless trash. Every man writes as much as he can, and quotes Montesquieu, and Hume, and Adam Smith, and speaks as if we were living in a country where people were free and governed themselves. Most of their papers might have been written by men who were never out of England, and their projects are nearly as applicable to that country as to India.[1]

Against the impersonal bureaucracy which Munro held to characterise the Cornwallis system, he supported a form of administration personal, human and near to the Indian population; one which was, he believed, in the Indian tradition, and easily intelligible to the ryot; for government was represented therein not by a multiplicity of officers with the power divided among them, but a by single officer, the collector and magistrate, who had powers to enquire, to judge, and to punish without the delay and intricacies of the Western legal process. Only in this way could the ryot be protected; and protection, in view of the relative ineffectiveness of political authority, was government's principal function. The ryots would not resist injustice by taking action through a British system of courts.

Our institutions here [wrote Munro] not resting on the same foundations as those of a free country, cannot be made to act in the same way. We cannot make the inanimate corpse perform the functions of the living body; we must, therefore, in making regulations here, think only of their probable effect in this country, not of what such regulations have or might have in England.[2]

Munro's was not a solitary voice. In countering the spirit of the Cornwallis system, he was joined by Malcolm, Elphinstone and Metcalfe; and despite differences of opinion among this group, most notably that between Malcolm and Metcalfe over the policy to be adopted towards the Indian states, there was a fundamental unity of thought, a common aim to conserve the richly varied original institutions of India society rather than to construct that society anew, an antipathy to 'regulation' and uniformity. It would be a mistake, therefore, to attempt to explain the sources of Munro's principles in terms of his particular upbringing and experience. Nevertheless, of the four men he had the longest experience of administration, and began it before the others. His career provided the field in which those principles which he held in common with Malcolm, Elphinstone and Metcalfe first had to be applied to actual administrative problems, and the result was the ryotwari settlement and the whole administrative system bound up with it. There is little discernible change in Munro's broad views. The development of 'the Munro system' was a development of the machinery of administration, of the protracted business of persuading the home government to order reforms and then to get them put into practice by the government at Fort St George. The Munro of the eighteen-twenties was not greatly changed from the Munro of the seventeen-nineties: he thought more favourably, or at least more tolerantly, of the Indian; he was perhaps even more scornful (if it was possible) of the knowledge of 'presidency men' than he had been, and more irascible where judicial servants were concerned. But in the development of his ideas on administrative practice, subordinate to his general philosophy, his actual experience was of the greatest importance.

After getting the idea of a ryotwari settlement from Read while they were working in the Baramahal, Munro's experience in Kanara assumed an importance which it might not otherwise have had. For Kanara was a part of south India where the revenue settlement had been made, historically, directly between the representatives of the government and the cultivator, and where the results of this appeared to have been beneficial. Twenty years after his work there, Munro wrote to Ravenshaw:

The object of the Rayetwar settlement is to make the Rayets of other districts like those of Canara—enjoying their lands as private property at a fixed rent— Some Rayets in every district are now in this condition—all may be brought to it gradually. It cannot be done suddenly—but it will require less time in proportion as the state of our finances may enable us to lower somewhat the present assessment.[1]

In the Ceded Districts he developed into a fine art the actual making of a ryotwari settlement, the surveying and assessing of the land; and the directions which he gave his Indian revenue servants for these tasks were circulated to other collectors by the Madras government for their instruction. For Munro, the ryotwari settlement was never an end in itself, nor did he hold out unreal hopes of what it might do. All hinged on the level of the assessment. If this was too high, no settlement could work. Munro recommended a 25 per cent reduction in the assessment of the Ceded Districts when he left in 1807. The government was not able to accept the recommendation, and the district was settled in village decennial leases. When these lapsed through non-payment, or expired at the end of the period, the district was economically much worse off than it had been before. Munro as governor made the reductions he had recommended as collector.

It was clear to Munro that too high an assessment would reduce all the population to a uniform level of poverty; and he was opposed both to poverty and to uniformity. He had a firm belief in the 'due gradation of society', which he believed in India partly took shape in the institution of caste. There was to be no egalitarianism in his ideal peasant community. The argument that, through a ryotwari settlement, he was levelling out the very variety he sought to maintain, was cutting ruthlessly through village inams and other customary payments, and was thus breaking down the village (which he in fact sought to keep as the central focus of Indian life) failed to move him. These were the results, he claimed, of the assessment remaining too high. They had begun in the time of Haidar and Tipu Sultan at least—indeed village institutions in south India appear to have declined in vigour through the eighteenth century, though the exact reasons for this are not entirely clear—and only by restoring the ryot to the position which Munro believed he had occupied as the cultivating proprietor, and lowering the assessment to a point where he obtained the profits of ownership rather than the returns of labour merely, could this decline be reversed. It is difficult without detailed studies of particular districts to decide how far Munro was right. A large proportion of the Madras territories was over-assessed, and when in the middle of the nineteenth century they were re-surveyed and the assessment lowered, the damage had been done.

Munro's ideas on the administration of justice were to a smaller extent than those on revenue practice the result of an appreciation of the virtues of Indian tradition. Rather, they resulted from the obvious faults of the Cornwallis system, both as far as Munro knew of its working in Bengal, and as demonstrated following its introduction into the Madras presidency. In the administration of civil justice, Munro believed, the Indians could hardly be said to have had any regular system. Decisions by various local officers, panchayats, the prince, or the court established near him, were 'irregular, and often corrupt and arbitrary', but in fact as much real justice was dispensed as in the British courts, with less delay and expense; 'for the native judges, whatever their irregularities were, had the great advantage of understanding their own language and their own code much better than ours are ever likely to do.'[1] The ways in which Munro thought the British should make use of these Indian judicial institutions have been discussed in the previous chapter. The district munsiffs were an immediate success. They relieved the zillah courts from a great mass of small suits, getting through a great deal of work, and the small number of appeals from their decisions suggested that this was performed in a way satisfactory to the inhabitants. Their success was perhaps one reason why the panchayats were not widely used, though Munro wrote that this was the result of the panchayat having been 'placed under so many restrictions . . . lest it become an instrument of abuse . . . as to deprive it of much of its utility'.[2] This is not borne out by his statement to Ravenshaw that the panchayats 'would do much more if the inhabitants had not a much quicker way of getting their causes settled by the district Munsifs. But if there were no Punchayets, the business of the Munsifs would not be so well done—because the Munsifs know that if they did not give satisfaction, the inhabitants would go to the Punchayets.'[3] One suspects, also, that the panchayats had not been as widespread and flourishing immediately before the British assumed control as Munro suggested. The authority given the patels as village munsiffs, to settle minor cases, was made but little use of. Here, again, it is not clear whether Munro had overestimated the amount of judicial work they had carried out formerly, or whether there was some reason for the failure of the judicial reforms to revive their usefulness in this capacity. Munro again attributed it to the success of the district munsiffs, as well as to the fact that the village munsiffs had been made amenable to the zillah courts, of which they were so afraid that they were very averse to undertaking any duty that might expose them to such cognizance.[1]

Munro's administrative methods were widely accepted by his contemporaries and influenced his successors.[2] Elphinstone corresponded regularly with him, sought his advice, and made use of a number of Madras-trained revenue servants—most notably William Chaplin, Hanumant Rao, who had been division sarishtadar in the Ceded Districts, and Lakshman Rao, for many years employed in revenue work under Munro—in the settlement of the large area of western India that was annexed to the Bombay presidency after the defeat of the Marathas.[3] He adopted the ryotwari settlement as the basis for the settlement in most of this territory, though he wrote that he was 'not democratic enough to insist on a ryotwar system'. 'I think', he continued, 'that the aristocracy of the country whether it consists of heads of villages or heads of zemindarees should be kept up but I also think its rights and the opposite rights of the ryots should be clearly defined and the latter especially effectually defended.'[4] But with Munro's efforts to administer justice through Indian institutions and methods he was in full agreement. In the north of India Metcalfe fought strongly against the extension of the Cornwallis system to the Ceded and Conquered Provinces. He never ceased to acknowledge Munro as master, and to pursue his ideal of a prosperous society of yeomen farmers enjoying a freehold property right; and during his administration of the Delhi territory he made the village communities the basis of the revenue settlement, and united the executive and magisterial functions in the person of the collector.[1]

With the utilitarians a new spirit entered Indian administration, in many ways reminiscent of that of Cornwallis. Yet there was much more in common between the administrative organisation of Munro and that of the utilitarians, than there was between the latter and the Cornwallis system. Munro and his school, Professor Stokes has written,

were largely in agreement with certain aspects of the Utilitarian viewpoint. The union of judicial and executive power in the collector; the simplification of the chaotic jungle of the law to a compact intelligible code which represented Indian custom; the prejudice for a ryotwar form of land settlement; and an accurate survey and record of landed rights—in all these reforms they were in agreement with the radical authoritarian strain in Utilitarian thought.[2]

In a sense Professor Stokes has phrased it the wrong way round. These were the aspects of the Munro system which the utilitarians took over and used as part of their own pattern of reform. It was Munro's authority that Bentinck invoked in support of his administrative reforms during 1829–31. He urged upon the home government, as the best means for improving the efficiency of the civil service, that they should

confirm and persevere in the system long since recommended by them to the Madras Government, upon the authority of Sir Thomas Munro, of uniting the appointments of collector and magistrate, of destroying the independence of each other of every officer employed in the same district, of making the collector's a great office, consisting of deputy collectors and joint magistrates and assistants, subordinate to one head, and acting upon the same system.[3]

The most lasting administrative results of the Munro system were the ryotwari settlement and the emphasis on strong executive rule. Adopted by the utilitarians, these played a part in creating the system of district officer and divisional commissioner, which, as the orthodox model for future British colonial government, successfully combined a strong executive arm with the rule of law.

But the spirit of 'the Munro system' did not long survive its founder. Munro's generation of administrators was the last whose object was 'to restore, to conserve, to continue, rather than to destroy, to innovate or to revolutionise'.[1] Yet, in the revenue collection and the local and district administration (the forms of which suggested a continuity with their Mughul predecessors), the policies they pursued, even with conservative intentions, released new social forces in rural India.

The main feature of British land policy was to define and record the rights of the agricultural classes and to guarantee the enjoyment of these rights through a system of courts. This underlying object no one questioned; although there was disagreement as to the rights of the numerous groups in rural society, of ryot, mirasdar and zamindar; and disagreement also about the nature of the courts and the laws they were to administer. There was little understanding of the relationship between traditional patterns of land tenure and the complex social ties of the village and district community. The cumulative effect of British policy was to facilitate the growth of individualism within rural societies. The registration of individual, saleable property-rights made possible a process of social mobility, created a context in which traditional institutions worked in new and sometimes startling ways. The changes that Munro looked for in Indian society were to be brought about (indeed, could only be brought about) slowly and cautiously. None the less, in the ryotwari system, and in the administrative reforms which helped to create a strong and active government, closely linked with the population through a large number of government servants, he laid the foundations on which a later generation of administrators with ideas of innovation, efficiency and improvement could base their reforms. The radical spirit did not preclude paternalism; but it transformed it. And the consciously assumed paternalism of later administrators produced an inflexibility of outlook, a refusal to recognise changes in Indian society, a reaction of irritation at the emergence of Indians who spurned the filial role. In considering Munro as an administrator, indeed, one salient thing is to be remembered: no less important than the views he held, or than the details of the ryotwari settlement or the village panchayat, is the fact that it was the Indians he ruled who looked upon him as their 'Father'.

NOTES

PAGE I

I Vincent T. Harlow, *The Founding of the Second British Empire 1763–1793*, vol. I, p. 4.

PAGE 4

I *The Fifth Report from the Select Committee on the Affairs of the East India Company. Ordered by the House of Commons to be printed, 28 July 1812* (hereafter cited as *Fifth Report*), p. 18.

PAGE 5

I Minute of Cornwallis, 18 September 1789, Charles Ross (ed.), *Correspondence of Marquess Cornwallis* (2nd ed.), vol. I, p. 562. All page references are to the 2nd edition.
2 Sir Richard Temple, *Men and Events of my Time in India*, p. 30.
3 H. R. C. Wright, 'Some Aspects of the Permanent Settlement in Bengal', in *Economic History Review*, 2nd series, vol. VII, no. 2, p. 212.

PAGE 6

I Cornwallis to Court of Directors, 18 August 1789, Charles Ross, *op. cit.* vol. I, p. 531.
2 Draft Despatch sent by the Court to the Board, I.O. Home Misc., vol. 486, pp. 58–9.

PAGE 7

I *Ibid.* The Directors resented also Wellesley's influence over Clive (the 2nd Lord Clive, governor of Madras 1798–1803) since it reduced the presidency of Fort St George to the status of a province.—B. B. Misra, *The Central Administration of the East India Company 1773–1834*, pp. 46–7.
2 Dundas to Wellesley, 4 September 1800; Wellesley Papers, Add. MS 37,275, f. 191; see also Revenue Despatch to Madras, 11 February 1801.
3 Such a system of settling the revenue by auction had been tried by Warren Hastings, and had frequently led to 'ruinous rack-renting and seriously impeded the general improvement of agriculture'.—B. B. Misra, *op. cit.* p. 180.
4 Revenue Despatch to Madras, 21 July 1802, para. 3.
5 Revenue Despatch to Madras, 10 April 1804, para. 22; ditto, 1 November 1805, para. 125.
6 Revenue Despatch to Madras, 24 August 1804, para. 22; ditto, 1 November 1805, para. 125.

PAGE 8

1 Munro to Board of Revenue, 15 August 1807, para. 6, MBRC, 4 February 1808.

PAGE 9

1 Munro to M. Elphinstone, 12 May 1818, G. R. Gleig, *The Life of Major General Sir Thomas Munro* (hereafter cited as Gleig), vol. 3, pp. 252–3.

2 Bentinck, Lord William Cavendish, 1774–1839. Entered the army in 1791, and served in the Netherlands and in North Italy with the Austrian forces in 1799–1801. Governor of Madras 1803–7, and subsequently envoy in Sicily 1811–13 with powers virtually of a governor; governor-general of India 1829–35.

3 P. Auber, *Rise and progress of the British Power in India*, vol. 2, p. 426.

4 *Ibid.* p. 444–5.

5 The Chairman and Deputy Chairman, Edward Parry and Charles Grant.

6 C. H. Philips, *The East India Company 1784–1834*, pp. 201–2.

PAGE 10

1 Grant to Bentinck, 21 March 1806, Bentinck Papers.

2 Revenue Despatch to Madras, 30 August 1809, para. 138. The Directors had previously expressed doubts as to how far a system of such 'extended detail' would answer satisfactorily for permanent use, in their Revenue Despatch to Madras, 6 November 1805, para. 37.

3 See below, Chapter 4.

PAGE 12

1 Charles Ross, *Correspondence of Marquess Cornwallis*, vol. 1, p. 346.

PAGE 14

1 Where not otherwise stated the following paragraph is based on the note on Read in I.O. Catalogue, Mackenzie Collection, pp. 435–7.

2 Munro to his father, 14 April 1793, Gleig, vol. 1, p. 147.

PAGE 15

1 Cornwallis to Read, 14 January 1792, Carfrae MSS, I.O. MS Eur. E 184, pp. 17–18.

2 Munro to his father, 14 April 1793, Gleig, vol. 1, pp. 147–8.

3 *Madras Courier*, 28 July 1791, quoted in I.O. Catalogue, Mackenzie Collection, p. 437.

PAGE 16

1 Munro to his father, September 1791, Gleig, vol. 1, p. 123.
2 Munro to his father, 28 April 1792, *ibid.* pp. 131–2.
3 The Board of Revenue at Fort St George, like that in Bengal, was set up as part of the general plan of the Court of Directors to administer through a series of Boards. Established in 1786, it consisted of three members drawn from the covenanted service presided over by a member of Council, and, subject to the final approbation and orders of government, was given general control over the whole field of revenue administration including settlement, collection and receipt of public revenues.

PAGE 17

1 J. W. B. Dykes, *Salem, an Indian Collectorate* (hereafter cited as *Salem*), p. 24.
2 Minute by C. D. White, MBRC, 25 March 1793, *Fifth Report*, appendix 14.
3 *Ibid.*
4 Read to Board of Revenue, June 1793, *Baramahal Records* (hereafter cited as *B.R.*), vol. 6, p. 1.
5 Read to Cornwallis, 1 July 1793, *B.R.*, vol. 6, pp. 20–57.
6 Read to Board of Revenue, June 1793, *B.R.*, vol. 6, pp. 1–20.
7 Read to Board of Revenue, June 1793, *ibid.* para. 17.

PAGE 18

1 Read to Board of Revenue, June 1793, *ibid.* paras. 52–5; see also Read to Cornwallis, 1 July 1793, *ibid.* para. 62.
2 Read to Board of Revenue, June 1793, *ibid.* para. 52.
3 *Ibid.* para. 54.
4 *Ibid.* para. 55; see also Read to Cornwallis, 1 July 1973, *ibid.* para. 63.
5 Read to Cornwallis, 1 July 1793, *B.R.*, vol. 6, pp. 20–57.

PAGE 19

1 Read to Board of Revenue, June 1793, paras. 10–11, 16, *B.R.*, vol. 6.
2 *Ibid.* para. 13.
3 *Ibid.* para. 15.
4 *Ibid.* para. 22.
5 *B.R.*, vol. 6, pp. 58–61.
6 *Ibid.*

PAGE 20

1 Dykes, *Salem*, p. 89.
2 Munro to Read, 31 July 1793; *B.R.*, vol. 6, pp. 60–1.

PAGE 21

1 Munro to Read, 31 July 1794, *B.R.*, vol. 1, pp. 220–1.
2 See Read to Board of Revenue, 30 December 1792, MBRC, 7 January 1793.
3 Read to Board of Revenue, 10 August 1794, para. 5, *B.R.*, vol. 1, pp. 203–4.
4 Munro to Read, 31 July 1794, *B.R.*, vol. 1, pp. 220–1.
5 Read to Board of Revenue, 12 September 1794, MBRC, 22 September 1794.
6 Munro to Captain Allen, 8 June 1794, Gleig, vol. 3, p. 92.
7 *Ibid.*
8 50,000 rupees equals approximately 18,000 pagodas [£7,200]. The gross revenue of the districts in 1793–4 was estimated by Munro to be 511,000 pagodas.—*Ibid.*

PAGE 22

1 Read to Board of Revenue, 10 August 1794, para. 3, *B.R.*, vol. 1, pp. 203–4; Munro to Captain Allen, 8 June 1794, Gleig, vol. 3, pp. 91–6; Minute of the Board of Revenue on Read's letter of 10 August 1794, MBRC, 25 August 1794.
2 Munro to Captain Allen, 8 June 1794, Gleig, vol. 3, pp. 95–6.
3 Read to Board of Revenue, 10 August 1794, paras. 8–9, *B.R.*, vol. 1, pp. 203–4.
4 Munro to Read, 31 July 1794, paras. 2–3, *B.R.*, vol. 1, pp. 220–1.
5 Read to Board of Revenue, 10 August 1794, para. 9, *B.R.*, vol. 1, pp. 203–4.

PAGE 23

1 MBRC, 25 August 1794.
2 Quoted in C. S. Srinivasachariar, 'The Settlement of Baramahal and Salem from the Records', in *Journal of Indian History*, vol. IV, part 1, p. 90.
3 Munro to Read, 31 July 1796, Madras Record Office, Public Sundries, vol. 121, p. 158.
4 'The average rent of the whole body of farmers is not more than ten pagodas [£4] each. I am pretty sure that there is not a man among them who is worth 500 l., and that, exclusive of their cattle, nine-tenths of them have not five pounds [12½ pagodas].'—Munro to his father, 10 May 1796, Gleig, vol. 1, p. 186.
5 Munro to Read, 31 July 1796, Madras Record Office, Public Sundries, vol. 121, p. 158.
6 Munro to Captain Allen, 8 June 1794, Gleig, vol. 3, p. 91.
7 Munro to his father, 31 January 1795, Gleig, vol. 1, p. 158.
8 Dykes, *Salem*, pp. 90–103.

PAGE 24

1 Munro to Read, 15 November 1796, Dykes, *Salem*, pp. 104–15.
2 *Ibid.* pp. 107–8.

PAGE 25
1 *Ibid.* p. 112.
2 *Ibid.* p. 115.
3 Dykes, *Salem,* pp. 119–36.

PAGE 26
1 *Ibid.* p. 122.
2 Munro to Read, 15 November 1796, Dykes, *Salem,* p. 107.
3 Munro to Read, 18 July 1797, Dykes, *Salem,* pp. 127–8.
4 *Ibid.* p. 125.
5 Munro to Read, 15 November 1796, Dykes, *Salem,* pp. 105–6.

PAGE 27
1 Munro to Read, 18 July 1797, Dykes, *Salem,* p. 126.
2 *Ibid.* pp. 134–5.
3 Read to his assistants, 25 July 1797; enclosed with Read to Board of Revenue, 16 August 1797, MBRC, 21 August 1797.
4 Munro to Read, 5 September 1797, Dykes, *Salem,* pp. 65–6.

PAGE 28
1 Munro to Read, 18 July 1797, Dykes, *Salem,* p. 136.
2 Munro to Read, 5 September 1797, Dykes, *Salem,* pp. 71–2.

PAGE 29
1 *Ibid.* pp. 164–6.
2 Munro to his father, 21 September 1798, Gleig, vol. 1, pp. 204, 205.
3 Munro to Read, 5 September 1797, Dykes, *Salem,* p. 142.

PAGE 30
1 Munro to his father, 21 September 1798, Gleig, vol. 1, p. 204. This letter closely echoes one from Munro to Read, 31 August 1798, Madras Record Office, Public Sundries, vol. 121, pp. 291–327. Dykes records that shortly before leaving the Baramahal in 1799 Munro heard a report that the ryotwari system was to be bound up into large farms, and that he wrote to Read condemning the proposal. He had, Dykes writes, 'altogether cast aside the lease hallucination, and boldly states his firm conviction that the ryotwarry system is the best for the country in its present state, and neither so intricate or troublesome to the collector as would appear at first sight'.—*Salem,* pp. 177–8. It is possible that the letter Dykes refers to is the one of 31 August 1798 mentioned above.
2 Board of Revenue to Read, 30 June 1797, MBRC, 30 June 1797.

3 Board of Revenue to Read, 4 June 1798, MBRC, 7 June 1798.
4 Minute of the Board of Revenue, 27 September 1798, MBRC, 27 September 1798.
5 Munro to his father, 21 September 1798, Gleig, vol. 1, p. 204.

PAGE 31
1 Minute of the Board of Revenue, 27 September 1798, MBRC, 27 September 1798.
2 N. Mukherjee, *The Ryotwari System in Madras 1792–1827*, p. 14.
3 Board of Revenue to the Governor-General in Council, 6 July 1799, MBRC, 6 July 1799.

PAGE 32
1 Read to Board of Revenue, 31 March 1793, MBRC, 8 April 1793. Munro also saw the implications for the everyday administration of justice of a zamindari settlement on the Bengal pattern. He wrote to Read: 'There has often been much discussion about Courts of Judicature to protect and secure the Inhabitants in the enjoyment of their Rights and property—but by the system of great Farms Government would itself at once deprive the great body of the farmers of the property they have in their lands, and place them under a few principal Landholders to be taxed at discretion. This act alone would comprehend more injustice and more causes of complaint than would otherwise arise in fifty years.'—Munro to Read, 31 August 1798, Madras Record Office, Public Sundries, vol. 121, pp. 294–5.
2 Munro to Read, 8 November 1795, *B.R.*, vol. 17, pp. 62–3.
3 Munro to Read, 27 July 1794, MBRC, 25 August 1794.
4 Munro to Read, 24 November 1798, Madras Record Office, Public Sundries, vol. 121, p. 345.

PAGE 33
1 *Ibid.*; also Munro to Read, 5 September 1797, Dykes, *Salem*, pp. 162–3.
2 *Ibid.*
3 *Ibid.*
4 *Ibid.*
5 Minute of the Board of Revenue, 5 January 1818, para. 156, MBRC.

PAGE 35
1 Sir John Malcolm, *The Political History of India*, vol. 1, p. 159.
2 R. Montgomery Martin (ed.), *The Despatches, Minutes and Correspondence of the Marquess Wellesley*, vol. 1, pp. xi–xii.
3 Wellesley to Court of Directors, 13 September 1799, quoted in Sir John Malcolm, *op. cit.* p. 218.

PAGE 36

1 Munro to his father, 2 August 1798, Gleig, vol. 3, pp. 108–9.
2 P. E. Roberts, *India under Wellesley*, p. 50.
3 Mark Wilks, *Historical Sketches of the South of India*, vol. 3, pp. 427–8.
4 R. Montgomery Martin (ed.), *The Despatches, Minutes and Correspondence of the Marquess Wellesley*, vol. 2, p. 12.

PAGE 37

1 Munro to his father, 6 August 1799, Gleig, vol. 1, p. 223.
2 Government to Board of Revenue, 6 July 1799, MBRC, 8 July 1799. Munro was placed 'on the same footing in point of salary and allowances as the other Collectors': i.e. his salary was 3,000 pagodas [£1,200] and he received an allowance of 1½ per cent on the revenue collected. At first he was to remain under the immediate authority of the Mysore Commissioners [*ibid.*], but in February 1800 he was placed under the orders of the Board of Revenue. Board of Revenue to Munro, 8 February 1800, MBRC, 10 February 1800.
3 Read, Alexander, writer 1796. Assistant under the collector of the Baramahal 1798; subsequently collector of the northern division of Kanara, and principal collector of Kanara.
4 Munro to his sister Erskine, 30 June 1799, Gleig, vol. 1, pp. 227–8.
5 Munro to Wellesley, 29 June 1799, R. Montgomery Martin (ed.), *The Despatches, Minutes and Correspondence of the Marquess Wellesley*, vol. 2, pp. 58–9.
6 Munro to his sister Erskine, 30 June 1799, Gleig, vol. 1, pp. 227–8.

PAGE 38

1 Munro to Board of Revenue, 31 May 1800, para. 2, MBRC, 28 August 1800.
2 Munro to Lieut.-Colonel Close, 16 June 1800, Carfrae MSS, I.O. MS Eur. E 184, pp. 36–52.

PAGE 39

1 Munro to Board of Revenue, 31 May 1800, para. 3, MBRC, 28 August 1800.
2 Munro to Close, 16 June 1800, Carfrae MSS, I.O. MS Eur. E 184, pp. 36–52.
3 *Ibid.*
4 Government to Close, 14 July 1800, MBRC, 31 July 1800.

PAGE 40

1 Munro, Memo. for Wellesley, December 1799, Wellesley Papers, Add. MS 13, 679, ff. 3–6.
2 Munro to Cockburn, 7 June 1800, Gleig, vol 1, pp. 248–51; see also Munro to Board of Revenue, 18 June 1800, MBRC, 3 July 1800.

3 Munro to Board of Revenue, 23 June 1800, MBRC, 7 July 1800.

4 Munro to Board of Revenue, 18 June 1800. MBRC, 3 July 1800.

5 Munro to Board of Revenue, 12 September 1800, MBRC, 29 September 1800.

6 Munro to Close, 16 June 1800, Carfrae MSS, I.O. MS Eur. E 184, pp. 36–52.

7 Munro to Close, 24 July 1800, enclosed with Close to Government, 2 August 1800, MPC, August 1800, p. 376.

8 Munro to Cockburn, undated, Gleig, vol. 1, p. 270.

PAGE 41

1 A. Wellesley to W. Kirkpatrick, 21 April 1800, Wellington (ed.), *Supplementary Despatches . . . of the Duke of Wellington*, vol. 1, pp. 529–30.

2 A. Wellesley to Kirkpatrick, 1 May 1800, *ibid.* pp. 552–3.

3 A. Wellesley to Kirkpatrick, 5 May 1800, *ibid.* pp. 559–60.

4 A. Wellesley to Close, 27 May 1800, *ibid.* pp. 573–5. See also Edward Thornton, *The History of the British Empire in India*, vol. 3, p. 115.

PAGE 42

1 A. Wellesley to Munro, 11 September 1800, Gleig, vol. 1, pp. 268–70.

2 Cockburn, Thomas, writer 1779. Member of the Board of Revenue 1795, second member of the Board 1800, and senior member 1801. Returned home in 1803.

3 Munro to Cockburn, 7 June 1800, Gleig, vol. 1, p. 250.

4 Munro to Lieut.-Colonel Wiseman, 8 September 1799, Carfrae MSS, I.O. MS Eur. E 183, pp. 1–4.

PAGE 43

1 Munro to Board of Revenue, 18 June 1800, MBRC, 3 July 1800.

2 A. Wellesley to Munro, 10 May 1800, Gleig, vol. 3, pp. 118–19.

3 Munro to Colonel Sartorius, 27 September 1799, Carfrae MSS, I.O. MS Eur. E 183, pp. 4–7.

4 Munro to Colonel Sartorius, 15 October 1799, Carfrae MSS, I.O. MS Eur. E 183, pp. 9–11.

PAGE 44

1 Munro to Close, 1 January 1800, Carfrae MSS, I.O. MS Eur. E 183, pp. 22–7.

2 Munro to Wellesley, June 1800, Wellesley Papers, Add. MS 13,679, ff. 36–7.

3 *Ibid.*

4 Board of Revenue to Munro, 8 February 1807, MBRC, 10 February 1800.

5 Munro to Board of Revenue, 27 February 1800, MBRC, 10 March 1800.

PAGE 45

1 *Ibid.*

2 Munro to Cockburn, 20 December 1799, Gleig, vol. 1, p. 241.

3 *Ibid.*

4 Munro to Cockburn, 28 February 1800, Gleig, vol. 1, pp. 243–4.

5 *Ibid.*

6 Munro to Cockburn, 7 October 1800, Gleig, vol. 1, p. 289.

7 Munro to Board of Revenue, 31 May 1800, MBRC, 28 August 1800. The following four pages are based on this report, quotations unless otherwise stated are from it, and paragraph numbers in square brackets in the text refer to it.

PAGE 46

1 Munro to Cockburn, 7 June 1800, Gleig, vol. 1, p. 248.

2 This is also emphasised in the report he wrote for the Governor-General: 'I perceived very soon after my arrival in [Kanara] . . . that it had for many years been going rapidly to decline and that the chief cause of it was an oppressive land rent. . . . To raise Canara and Sondah from the condition into which they are fallen and to enable them to avail themselves of their natural advantages and to reach a higher degree of natural prosperity than ever they enjoyed before nothing more is necessary than to reduce the land rent to its ancient standard.'—Munro to Wellesley, 25 April 1800, Wellesley Papers, Add. MS 13,679, ff. 7–9. I give further references to this report simply under the date.

3 Munro to Read, 5 September 1797, Dykes, *Salem*, p. 164. See above p. 28.

4 Munro to Wellesley, 25 April 1800.

PAGE 47

1 'The Arthasastra suggests one quarter or even one third [of the crop as the sarkar share] for fertile lands; there is some reason to believe that one quarter was the proportion generally levied. . . . The tax was usually paid in kind . . . but in the middle ages, especially in the South, many villages had commuted their land tax for a regular annual cash payment.'—A. L. Basham, *The Wonder that was India*, p. 107.

2 Munro to Wellesley, 25 April 1800.

PAGE 48

1 The figures given are Munro's. Whether they represented fourteenth- or nineteenth-century valuations he does not make clear.

1 Munro to Cockburn, 13 July 1800, Gleig, vol. 1, pp. 251–2. In forwarding Munro's report to Government the Board said there was need for 'further investigation and elucidation'.—Board of Revenue to Government, 28 August 1800, MBRC, 28 August 1800.

2 Munro to Cockburn, 13 July 1800, Gleig, vol. 1, pp. 251–2. The Board agreed with this recommendation. Board of Revenue to Government, 28 August 1800, MBRC, 28 August 1800.

3 Munro to Board of Revenue, 19 November 1800, MBRC, 11 December 1800. In the following four pages paragraph numbers in square brackets in the text refer to this report.

1 Munro's Journal, 21 January 1800, Gleig, vol. 1, pp. 280–1.

2 Munro to Board of Revenue, 4 May 1800, para. 7, MBRC, 15 May 1800. This survey was approved by the government and the Superintendent of the Surveying School was instructed to assist Munro 'with persons better able to conduct the service than those now employed'.—Government to Board of Revenue, 31 May 1800, MBRC, 9 June 1800.

3 Munro to Cockburn, 7 October 1800, Gleig, vol. 1, p. 291.

1 Munro to Board of Revenue, 21 August 1800, MBRC, 4 September 1800.

2 See above p. 28.

1 Ravenshaw, John Goldsborough, writer 1796. Head assistant to the collector of Dindigul 1799. Following his appointment to the northern division of Kanara, he was principal collector in the southern division of Arcot. He returned home in 1813, and in 1819 was elected a Director of the East India Company.

2 Munro to Read and Ravenshaw, 9 December 1800, Carfrae MSS, I.O. MS Eur. E 183, pp. 56–75.

3 Munro to Cockburn, 28 February 1800, Gleig, vol. 1, p. 245.

4 Munro to Cockburn, 13 July 1800, Gleig, vol. 1, p. 252.

5 *Ibid.*

1 Munro to Read, 16 June 1801, Gleig, vol. 3, pp. 160–3.

2 The Madras Government wrote that his report of 30 May 1800 was 'one of the ablest . . . which had passed under their observation'.—Revenue Letter

from Madras, 9 October 1800, paras. 63–70. The Court's satisfaction is expressed in Revenue Despatch to Madras, 30 August 1804, paras. 24–6.

3 Munro to Cockburn, 7 October 1800, Gleig, vol. 1, pp. 288–9.

PAGE 55

1 Munro to Webbe, 21 November 1800, Wellesley Papers, Add. MS 13,629, ff. 296–8.

2 Clive to Wellesley, 30 October 1800, I.O. Home Misc., vol. 462, pp. 189–203.

3 Government to Munro, 24 October 1800, MSC, 23 October 1800.

Cochrane, James, writer 1794. After three years in the Ceded Districts he was appointed collector of Ramnad and Tinnevelly, 1803, and then judge and magistrate of the northern division of Kanara. Following a period at home he was appointed a member of the Board of Revenue, 1814, president of the Board of Revenue and acting member of Council, 1824, and finally second judge of the Sadr Adalut, 1825–30.

Stodart, Alexander, writer 1789. Assistant under the collector of Dindigul, 1796, and under the collector of the third division of Vizagapatam, 1798. His career was cut short by ill-health. At home from 1803–7, he died shortly after his return to Madras.

Thackeray, William, writer 1793. After the Ceded Districts was appointed judge in the zillah of Masulipatam, 1803, junior member of the Board of Revenue, 1806, chief secretary to government, 1810–13. He was at home, 1813–17, and following his return to Madras became collector and magistrate of Bellary, 1818, third judge of the Sadr Adalut, member of the Council, and president of the Board of Revenue, 1820. Died in January 1823.

PAGE 56

1 Munro to Government, 18 January 1801, MPC, 27 January 1801.

2 Webbe, Josiah, writer 1783. Secretary to government of Madras 1797, chief secretary to government 1800. In 1801 he was appointed resident at the court of the raja of Mysore, but did not take up the position. In 1804 he became resident at Nagpur, and died the following year. Lord Clive leant heavily on Webbe's advice in the transaction of all business at Fort St George.

3 Munro to Webbe, 18 March 1801, Wellesley Papers, Add. MS 13,629, ff. 356–9.

4 Munro to Webbe, 24 November 1800, ibid. ff. 300–2.

5 Munro to Webbe, 10 December 1800, ibid. ff. 312–15.

6 Munro's apprehensions were justified in the case of Stodart, who, while admittedly ill, had, Munro wrote, 'none of those [qualifications] which will ever enable him to manage a Country' and knew 'nothing of the Country language'.—Munro to Webbe, 5 February 1801, I.O. MS Eur. F 18, pp. 23–6.

Stodart's health did not recover and seven months later his resignation was accepted by the Governor in Council.—Board of Revenue to Munro, 18 September 1801, MBRC, 17 September 1801.

1 Munro to Board of Revenue, 29 June 1802, MBRC, 15 July 1802.

2 Board of Revenue to Munro, 30 September 1802, MBRC, 30 September 1802.

1 *Ibid.*

2 Munro to Board of Revenue, 3 November 1802, MBRC, 25 November 1802.

3 *Ibid.*; and Board of Revenue to Munro, 3 December 1802, MBRC, 25 November 1802.

4 Government to Board of Revenue, 19 February 1803, MRC, 22 February 1803.

5 Munro to Webbe, 8 December 1800, Wellesley Papers, Add. MS 13,629, ff. 304–6. A fortnight later he wrote that from 'the northern Districts the famine . . . is said to have swept off half the Inhabitants'.—Munro to Webbe, 20 December 1800, *ibid.* ff. 316–19.

1 Munro to Board of Revenue, 12 August 1801, para. 15, MBRC, 31 August 1801.

2 Munro to Court of Directors, 12 July 1808, I.O. Misc. Letters Received, vol. 118, no. 196.

1 Munro to Board of Revenue, 20 March 1802, paras. 4–5, MBRC, 1 November 1802.

2 *Ibid.* para. 9.

3 Munro to Government, 21 November 1800, MPC, December 1800; Munro to Government, 13 January 1801, MPC, 27 January 1801; Munro to Wellesley, 30 August 1801, Wellesley Papers, Add. MS 13,679, ff. 62–4.

4 Government to Munro, 25 December 1800, MPC, December 1800.

1 Clive to Wellesley, 30 October 1800, I.O. Home Misc., vol. 462, pp. 189–203.

2 Munro to Webbe, 21 November 1800, Wellesley Papers, Add. MS 13,629, ff. 296–8.

1 Munro to Webbe, 1 January 1801, *ibid.* ff. 332–4.

2 Munro to Government, 27 March 1801, MPC, 3 April 1801; Munro to Webbe, 6 April 1801, Wellesley Papers, Add. MS 13,629, ff. 362–6; Munro to Board of Revenue, 20 March 1802, para. II, MBRC, 1 November 1802.

3 Munro to Government, 18 March 1801, MPC, 3 April 1801.

4 Government to Campbell, 3 April 1801, *ibid.*

5 Munro to Board of Revenue, 22 February 1805, MBRC, 4 March 1805.

PAGE 63

1 Campbell to Government, 10 May 1801, MPC, 26 May 1801.

2 Colonel Moneypenny to Campbell, 10 May 1801, enclosed *ibid.*

3 Munro to Government, 8 January 1802, MRC, 8 January 1802; Munro to Board of Revenue, 20 March 1802, paras. 12–14, MBRC, 15 July 1802.

PAGE 64

1 G. Buchan to Henry Dundas, 17 February 1802, Melville Papers, John Rylands Library, Eng. MSS 674, MS 275.

2 Munro to Webbe, 10 April 1801, Wellesley Papers, Add. MS 13,629, ff. 367–74.

3 Government to Campbell, 28 May 1801, MPC, 26 May 1801.

4 Board of Revenue to Munro, 28 March 1803, MBRC, 28 March 1803.

5 Minute of Board of Revenue, MBRC, 8 June 1801.

6 Board of Revenue to Government, 1 November 1802, para. 19, MBRC, 1 November 1802.

7 It is doubtful just how far it was within the Board's power to give instructions to Munro relating to the poligars. When the administration of the revenue and of the civil government of the Ceded Districts was placed under their control, political matters 'arising from . . . the description and power of the different Chieftains situated within the limits of those provinces' were reserved to the control of the Governor in Council. Government to Munro, 4 April 1801, MPC, 3 April 1801.

8 Revenue Despatch to Madras, 10 April 1804, paras. 19–21.

PAGE 65

1 Revenue Despatch to Madras, 15 May 1805, paras. 40–1.

2 Revenue Despatch to Madras, 10 April 1804, para. 21.

3 Munro to Bentinck, 15 November 1804, Bentinck Papers.

PAGE 66

1 Munro to Bentinck, 11 March 1805, Bentinck Papers.

2 Munro to Board of Revenue, 22 February 1805, MBRC, 4 March 1805 (transmitted to the Court of Directors, without comment by the Madras Government, Revenue Letter from Madras, 8 March 1805, paras. 178–9).

3 *Ibid.*

4 Revenue Despatch to Madras, 2 July 1806, paras. 80–3.

PAGE 67

1 *Ibid.* para. 81.

2 Munro made this claim only in a private letter, and did not repeat it in his letter to the Board of Revenue in which he sought to justify his actions. There is no proof for this apart from Munro's word: but it is clear that Webbe, anyway, can have been under no doubt whatsoever as to Munro's views towards the poligars. As there are no letters recorded from the Madras government which criticise Munro's poligar policy—until 1805, that is, when Bentinck considered Munro has in one instance been too lenient (Bentinck to Munro, 14 February 1805, Bentinck Papers)—on those grounds alone, Munro would have appeared justified in assuming that he had the support of government.

3 Bentinck to Munro, 29 October 1805, Bentinck Papers.

4 Munro to Bentinck, 12 May 1806, Bentinck Papers.

PAGE 69

1 Munro to Board of Revenue, 28 June 1802, MBRC, 8 July 1802.

2 Clive to Wellesley, 30 October 1800, I.O. Home Misc., vol. 462, pp. 189–203.

3 Munro to Wellesley, 10 July 1802, Wellesley Papers, Add. MS 13,679, ff. 66–8.

4 Munro's instructions to his assistants, 31 December 1800, Erskine MSS, I.O. MS Eur. D 31, pp. 113–32.

5 Munro to Wellesley, 10 July 1802.

PAGE 70

1 *Ibid.*

2 Munro to his assistants, 10 August 1801, Erskine MSS, I.O. MS Eur. D 31, pp. 189–93.

3 Munro to Board of Revenue, 3 November 1802, MBRC, 25 November 1802.

4 Munro to his assistants, 30 September 1802, enclosed with Munro to Board of Revenue, 2 May 1803, MBRC, 19 May 1803.

PAGE 71

1 *Ibid.*

2 Copies of the instructions are enclosed with Munro to Board of Revenue, 26 July 1807, MBRC, 24 August 1807.

PAGE 72

1 Munro to Board of Revenue, 26 July 1807, MBRC, 24 August 1807.
2 *Ibid.*

PAGE 73

1 The establishment of a special commission rather than leaving the settlement to the Board of Revenue is reported in a letter from G. Buchan to Henry Dundas to have been the result of personal animosity, which, not for the first time, bedevilled government in Madras. Lord Clive wished to return to England in 1802 but remained, at Wellesley's urging, partly because of the interruption to the permanent settlement which would have resulted from his departure; for, should he have adhered to his resolution, Cockburn (senior member of the Board of Revenue) declared his intention of resigning his seat at the Board. This was because he would not work with Place, who had been appointed to the Board by the Court of Directors, although while collector in the Jagir he had 'indulged himself in very indecorous language towards the Board of Revenue, while acting under its authority'. The commission was therefore set up 'to consist of Mr Petrie, Mr Cockburn and Mr Webbe, by which means Mr Cockburn is relieved from any immediate connection with the Board of Revenue though still a nominal member of it.'—G. Buchan to Henry Dundas, 17 February 1802, Melville Papers, John Rylands Library, Eng. MSS 674, MS 275.

PAGE 74

1 Governor-General in Council to Madras Government, 19 July 1804.— I.O. Tracts, vol. 465.
2 Eric Stokes, *The English Utilitarians and India*, p. 8.
3 Lord Clive, 'with the purest and most honourable intentions that ever actuated the mind of any person, has it cannot be denied little disposition for public affairs, and in the most ordinary details of business leans upon the support of others.'—G. Buchan to Henry Dundas, 17 February 1802, Melville Papers, John Rylands Library, Eng. MSS 674, MS 275.
4 Bentinck to Castlereagh, 16 October 1804, Bentinck Papers. Bentinck is misleading when he says that he urged Wellesley 'to permit the general introduction of Courts of Justice'. That, in fact, it was rather a case of his giving his full support to a policy on which Wellesley had already decided is made clear by his letter to Wellesley in which he writes: 'The flagrant abuse of authority in the Southern Division of Arcot & in Tanjoor made me anxious for the establishment of Zillah Courts in every part of the Country. It is impossible not to concur in every part of that excellent letter in the Judicial Department containing your Lordship's orders for the introduction

of the Judicial System.'—Bentinck to Wellesley, 9 September 1804, Wellesley Papers, Add. MS 13,634, ff. 198–9.

1 Munro's Comments on Wellesley's letter to Bentinck, Wellesley Papers, Add. MS 13,679, ff. 73–5.
2 *Ibid.* Bentinck did not agree with this argument. 'It is the fashion here I find', he wrote to Wellesley, 'to believe that the Courts will impede the Collection of the Revenues. They will certainly interfere with unjustifiable & unwarranted acts of arbitrary power on the part of the Revenue inferior servants. In the existence of such a check, the Collector ought to rejoice. There can be no collision of Authority. The Collector must find relief & assistance from the Court in the just discharge of his duty.'—Bentinck to Wellesley, 9 September 1804, Wellesley Papers, Add. MS 13,634, ff. 198–9.
3 Munro's Comments on Wellesley's letter to Bentinck, Wellesley Papers, Add. MS 13,679, ff. 73–5.

1 Minute of the Board of Revenue, 27 December 1804, MBRC, 27 December 1804.
2 Munro, 'Remarks on the Proposed Regulations of the Board of Revenue', 13 May 1805, MBRC, 13 June 1805.
3 *Ibid.*
4 Munro to Board of Revenue, 13 May 1805, MBRC, 13 June 1805.
5 Petrie, William, writer 1765, factor 1771, junior merchant 1774, senior merchant 1776, member of the Council and president of the Board of Revenue 1800. He was acting governor, following Bentinck's departure, from 11 September 1807 to 24 December 1807, and subsequently was governor of Prince of Wales Island, 1809–16.

1 Munro to Petrie, 22 May 1805, Wellesley Papers, Add. MS 13,679, ff. 84–5.
2 'In the opinion of the Board, the formation of Leasehold Estates would greatly impede the attainment of authentic information of the resources of the country, and obstruct in a still greater degree the survey and assessment, which the Board entirely concur with his Lordship [Bentinck] in considering as the ground-work of an equitable settlement in perpetuity'.—'Replies by the Board of Revenue to Bentinck's Queries', 15 June 1805, MRC, 20 June 1805.
3 Minute of Bentinck, 19 June 1805, MRC, 20 June 1805. See also Board of Revenue to Munro, 3 September 1805, MBRC, 2 September 1805.

4 Minute of Bentinck, 19 June 1805, MRC, 20 June 1805. See also P. Auber, *Rise and Progress of the British Power in India*, vol. 2, p. 426.

5 'Replies by the Board of Revenue to Bentinck's Queries', 15 June 1805, MRC, 20 June 1805.

6 Minute of Bentinck, 19 June 1805, MBRC, 20 June 1805.

7 Bentinck's circular letter to collectors, 27 May 1805, Bentinck Papers.

PAGE 78

1 Minute of Bentinck, 22 January 1806, *Fifth Report*, appendix 31.

2 Thackeray's Memoir was submitted by Bentinck to his Council, 29 April 1806. It is printed in *Fifth Report*, appendix 31.

3 Munro had written his first long report advocating a permanent ryotwari settlement in the Ceded Districts the previous year.—Munro to Board of Revenue, 25 August 1805, MBRC, 26 September 1805. As instructions had just been sent to the collectors that the existing forms of management should be continued until the survey was completed, the Board felt it was 'unnecessary to take his propositions into immediate consideration'.—Minute of Board of Revenue, MBRC, 26 September 1805.

4 Minute of Bentinck, 29 April 1806, *Fifth Report*, appendix 31. Wellesley certainly did not share this view of Bentinck's, having written 'It can never be desirable that the government itself shall act as proprietor of lands, and should collect the rents from the immediate cultivators of the soil. . . . If any differences should arise between landholders and the tenants regarding [their] engagements or usages, the courts of judicature will form the proper tribunals for deciding such differences. Those questions are of private right, in which the executive authority cannot interfere consistent with justice, policy, or its own interests'.—Governor-General in Council to Madras Government, 19 July 1804, para. 31, I.O.L. Tracts, vol. 465.

5 Minute of Bentinck, 28 November 1806, *Fifth Report*, appendix 31.

6 Munro to Bentinck, 10 June 1805, Bentinck Papers.

7 Minute of Bentinck, 28 November 1806, *Fifth Report*, appendix 31.

PAGE 79

1 Revenue letter from Madras, 21 October 1806, paras. 302–5. It is doubtful if the Court of Directors would have approved Munro's appointment. They expressed surprise that Bentinck 'should have even hinted at such an arrangement as that for placing a military officer however highly we may think of the merits of that officer at the Board of Revenue'.—Revenue Despatch to Madras, 30 August 1809, para. 101.

2 Wallace, John, writer 1792. Head assistant to the collector of Tanjore 1800,

collector of Trichinopoly 1801, principal collector of Tanjore and Trichinopoly 1805, second member of the Board of Revenue 1813. Died August 1814,
in Madras.

3 Bentinck to Petrie, undated, Bentinck Papers.

4 Minute of Bentinck, 28 November 1806, *Fifth Report*, appendix 31. In reply
to a letter from Munro in which he had apparently asked for Bentinck's
assistance in getting him appointed to the Hyderabad Residency, Bentinck
wrote: 'I should be sorry that you left the Ceded Districts till the Survey
Assess. and subsequent settlement are completed. After that your services
would be thrown away by your remaining in your present situation. I should
then be happy to see you in the Appointment of the greatest trust in the
Country. I have been sincere in the good opinion I have always expressed of
your services and if the opportunity offers I will do you all the good in my
power. You deserve from the Government and from the Company every
pecuniary and honourable distinction which they have to bestow.'—Bentinck
to Munro, 2 December 1805, Bentinck Papers.

5 Munro to Board of Revenue, 25 August 1805, MBRC, 26 September 1805.
I give further references to this report simply under the date.

6 Munro to Board of Revenue, 15 August 1807, MBRC, 4 February 1808
(printed in *SRJ*, vol. 1, pp. 94–8). I give further references to this report
simply under the date.

7 Munro to Board of Revenue, 25 August 1805, para. 2.

PAGE 80

1 Munro was as ready as any other administrator to generalise from his particular
experience. To some extent he found in his investigations what he set out to
look for: with many another conservative, he sought to conserve institutions
which existed more clearly in his mind than in society before him. In assessing
the importance of Munro's views in the formation of policy, their accuracy is
not necessarily the most relevant factor to consider; yet it is worth noting that
his arguments took the form that existing institutions, having been produced by society and having stood the test of time, were the most efficient.

2 Munro to Board of Revenue, 25 August 1805, para. 7.

3 See pp. 85–6.

4 See pp. 51–2.

PAGE 81

1 Munro to Board of Revenue, 25 August 1805, paras. 8–10; Munro to Board of
Revenue, 15 August 1807, paras. 6–10.

2 Munro to Board of Revenue, 25 August 1805, para. 12.

PAGE 82

1 Munro to Board of Revenue, 15 August 1807, para. 3.

PAGE 83

1 *Ibid.* para. 11.

2 *Ibid.* paras. 20–6.

PAGE 84

1 *Ibid.* para. 24.

2 Hodgson, John, writer 1792, assistant under the collector in the Jagir 1796, and collector in the Jagir 1799. Secretary in the judicial and revenue department 1800, and secretary to the Special Commission for the permanent settlement 1802. In 1803 he became junior member of the Board of Revenue, in 1806 second member, and he resumed the latter position after being in Britain from 1808–12. In 1813 he became senior member of the Board, in 1819 president, and a member of the Council. He left Madras in 1821.

PAGE 85

1 Report of the Board of Revenue, 25 April 1808, MBRC.

2 'Permanent Settlement and Ryotwar at Madras, by a Madras Covenanted Servant' (William Thackeray), undated (*c.* 1814), I.O. Home Misc., vol. 530, pp. 291–338.

PAGE 86

1 Campbell, Alexander Duncan, writer 1807, deputy secretary of the Board of Revenue 1812, and secretary of the Board 1817. Subsequently held a number of revenue and judicial appointments, finishing as first judge of the Sadr Adalat in 1842.

2 Evidence of A. D. Campbell before the Select Committee of the House of Commons, P.P., 1831–2 (735—III) XI. 1, pp. 202.

PAGE 87

1 B. S. Baliga, 'The Influence of the Home Government on Land Revenue and Judicial Administration in the Presidency of Fort William in Bengal from 1807 to 1822' (unpublished thesis, London, 1933), p. 317.

2 Dissent of S. Davis, 9 August 1817, I.O. Appendix to Court Minutes, vol. 3. That Munro himself was not immune to this attitude is shown by his remark to Cumming that 'the [Bengal] Judicial System is not what [Cornwallis] expected it to be'. Munro to Cumming, 30 November 1813, I.O. Home Misc., vol. 529, p. 299.

3 Dissent of S. Davis, 9 August 1817, I.O. Appendix to Court Minutes, vol. 3.

PAGE 88

1 S. Davis to M. Elphinstone, undated (*c*. 1818), quoted in Kenneth Ballhatchet, 'The Authors of the Fifth Report of 1812', in *Notes and Queries*, vol. CCII (1957), pp. 477–8.

2 [James Cumming], *Brief Notice of the Services of Mr Cumming*, pp. 63–70 (note).

3 Evidence of the Right Hon. T. P. Courtenay before the Select Committee of the House of Commons, P.P., 1831–2 (735—I) IX. I, p. 36.

4 [James Cumming], *Brief Notice of the Services of Mr Cumming*, pp. 4–5.

5 James Cumming, I.O. Home Misc., vol. 593, facing p. 1.

6 *Ibid.*

PAGE 89

1 *Ibid.*

2 I.O. Home Misc., vol. 593, pp. 1–120.

3 Dundas's letter in reply, 23 January 1809, is listed in an index of his correspondence, Melville Papers, John Rylands Library, Eng. MSS 698, but neither Munro's letter nor a draft of the reply is in the collection.

4 James Cumming, I.O. Home Misc., vol. 530, pp. 469–70.

5 Cumming described it as 'a Code the *essence* of which, by a perverted order of things, consisted for the greater part of a *multitude* of *forms* and *observances* and restrictions of the power of the collector which must have not only thrown the greatest difficulties and impediments in his way in the administration of the Ryotwar plan but have rendered it next to impossible, duly to conduct it without acting *in the very teeth of those Regulations.*'—*Ibid.*

PAGE 90

1 James Cumming, 'Memoir on . . . the Judicial System . . . of Fort St George', I.O. Home Misc., vol. 593, pp. 1–120.

2 *Ibid.*

3 *Ibid.*

4 'The pleadings in the suit, are a matter of record (as well as the evidence of witnesses), and they proceed by the Petition Replication and Rejoinder, Supplemental Answer and Reply. All this is perfectly new to the Natives, to whom Justice was used to be administered according to very simple rules, and, in a summary manner.'—*Ibid.*

5 Colonel Leith to the Chairman of the Court of Directors, 23 January 1808, quoted by Cumming, *ibid.*

PAGE 91

1 *Ibid.*

2 *Ibid.*

3 James Cumming, I.O. Home Misc., vol. 530, p. 457.

4 James Cumming, 'Memoir on ... the Judicial System ... of Fort St George', I.O. Home Misc., vol. 593, pp. 1–120.

5 James Cumming, I.O. Home Misc., vol. 530, pp. 458–9.

6 See Munro to Cumming, 30 November 1813, I.O. Home Misc., vol. 693, p. 150.

7 [James Cumming], *Brief Notice of the Services of Mr Cumming*, pp. 63–70 (note).

PAGE 92

1 E.g. see John Malcolm to W. F. Elphinstone, 4 December 1813, W. F. Elphinstone Papers, I.O. MS Eur. F 89, Box 2B.

2 This was also true of the Bengal section of the report on which Davis later commented: 'I wrote ... with the view to *open eyes* and excite further enquiry for I durst not go as far with truth as I might have gone for fear of exciting clamour among the admirers, from theory, of the existing system.'— S. Davis to M. Elphinstone, undated (*c.* 1818), quoted in Kenneth Ballhatchet, 'The Authors of the Fifth Report of 1812', in *Notes and Queries*, vol. CCII (1957), pp. 477–8.

3 *Fifth Report*, pp. 123–4.

4 *Fifth Report*, p. 152.

5 *Fifth Report*, p. 166.

PAGE 93

1 Evidence of the Right Hon. T. P. Courtenay before the Select Committee of the House of Commons, P.P., 1831–2 (735—1) IX. 1, p. 203.

2 W. F. Elphinstone and John Inglis, 7 June 1816, I.O. Secret Committee of Correspondence.

3 H. R. C. Wright, *East-Indian Economic Problems of the Age of Cornwallis and Raffles*, pp. 97–8.

4 Committee of Correspondence, 15 March 1814, I.O. Correspondence Reports, vol. 39, pp. 111–12.

5 Dissent of T. Hudlestone, 1 April 1814, I.O. Appendix to Court Minutes, vol. 3.

PAGE 94

1 John Malcolm to W. F. Elphinstone, 4 December 1813, W. F. Elphinstone Papers, I.O. MS Eur. F 89, Box 2B.

2 Dissent of S. Davis, 9 August 1817, I.O. Appendix to Court Minutes, vol. 3.

3 Dissent of S. Davis, 9 August 1817, *ibid.*

4 Melville Papers, John Rylands Library, Eng. MSS 693, MS 2017. Dundas had written to the 'Chairs' on 15 December 1807 and 9 January 1809, on the

NOTES

'necessity for adopting measures for conducting [the correspondence with India] with a greater degree of regularity'.—I.O. Minutes of the Board of Control, vol. 4, p. 137.

5 As these replies to Wellesley's queries were not taken into consideration by the Court in any despatch to India, copies were not even sent to the Board of Control.—Cumming, 'Memoir on ... the Judicial System ... of Fort St George', I.O. Home Misc., vol. 593, pp. 1–120.

PAGE 95

1 Cumming, I.O. Home Misc., vol. 692, facing p. 1.
2 Charles Grant, Jun., House of Commons, 31 May 1813, *Hansard*, vol. xxvi, p. 441.
3 Lord Grenville, House of Lords, 16 March 1813, *Hansard*, vol. xxv, p. 133.
4 Rickards was on the Bombay establishment from 1789 till 1811. After filling various revenue appointments he became private secretary to Jonathan Duncan during Duncan's governorship, and after that was successively commissioner in Malabar, chief secretary to the Bombay Government, principal collector of Malabar, and finally a member of the Government of Bombay.
5 Rickards, House of Commons, 2 June 1813, *Hansard*, vol. xxvii, pp. 1105–35.

PAGE 96

1 Grant, House of Commons, 2 June 1813, *Hansard*, vol. xxvi, p. 519. Grant was not disinterested, having played a part in making the decisions on the Cornwallis settlement and having, himself, drafted the despatch to Bengal on that subject.—Henry Morris, *The Life of Charles Grant*, pp. 169–71.

PAGE 97

1 Grant, House of Commons, 28 June 1813, *Hansard*, vol. xxvi, p. 935.
2 Grant, 2 June 1813, *Hansard*, vol. xxvi, p. 519.
3 Henry Thornton, House of Commons, 19 June 1813, *Hansard*, vol. xxvi, p. 545.
4 Lord Grenville, House of Lords, 16 March 1813, *Hansard*, vol. xxv, pp. 133–4. He made similar remarks on 9 April, *ibid.* pp. 745–7.
5 Rickards, House of Commons, 14 June 1813, *Hansard*, vol. xxvii, p. 1137.
6 21 December 1813, I.O. Letters from the Board of Control to the East India Company, vol. 4, p. 24. Those present at the meeting of the Board when this was voted were Buckinghamshire, Thomas Wallace and John Sullivan.—I.O. Minutes of the Board of Control, vol. 5, p. 128. These three were the only members to attend meetings of the Board regularly.—*Ibid.* passim.
7 24 December 1813, I.O. Letters from the East India Company to the Board of Control, vol. 5, pp. 27–9.

PAGE 98

1 18 January 1814, I.O. Letters from the Board of Control to the East India Company, vol. 4, pp. 59–60.

2 I.O. Court Minutes, vol. 121A, pp. 1234–66.

3 I.O. Madras Draft Despatches, vol. 21, Judicial Draft 123.

4 20 April 1814, I.O. Letters from the Board of Control to the East India Company, vol. 4, pp. 59–60.

5 Dissent of T. Hudleston, 11 May 1814, I.O. Appendix to Court Minutes, vol. 3.

6 Judicial Draft No. 123, para. 13, I.O. Madras Draft Despatches, vol. 21.

PAGE 99

1 Para. 15, *ibid.*

2 Dissent of T. Hudleston, 11 May 1814, I.O. Appendix to Court Minutes, vol. 3.

3 Judicial Draft No. 123, para. 61.

4 Munro, Memoir on the Judicial System, Edinburgh, 10 September 1808, National Library of Scotland, MS 12, pp. 187–9.

PAGE 100

1 S. Toone to Warren Hastings, 1 September 1813, Hastings Papers, Add. MS 29,188, f. 241.

2 Minute by the Chairman and Deputy Chairman (Grant and Reid), I.O. Secret Committee of Correspondence, 9 April 1816.

3 Cumming, 'On the Practicability of a Diminution in the Charges of the Judicial Department', I.O. Home Misc., vol. 529, p. 545.

4 Evidence of the Right Hon. T. P. Courtenay before the Select Committee of the House of Commons, P.P., 1831–2 (735—I) IX. 1, p. 35.

PAGE 101

1 C. H. Philips, *The East India Company*, p. 194.

2 *Ibid.* p. 204.

PAGE 102

1 Judicial Despatch to Madras, 4 May 1814.

2 Munro to Government, 24 December 1814, *SRJ*, vol. 2, pp. 292–6.

3 'The Government, with its secretaries, the Sudder Adawlut, and its register, and every member of the Board of Revenue, excepting Cochrane, are hostile to every thing in the shape of the rayetwar system.'—Munro to Cumming, 1 March 1815, Gleig, vol. 1, pp. 426–9.

4 Hugh Elliot, 1752–1830, was a younger brother of the 1st Earl of Minto. He was educated at school in Paris (where he is said to have been a friend of the schoolboy Mirabeau) and at Christ Church, Oxford. From 1773 he held various diplomatic positions in Europe until he was finally recalled from Naples, after having attempted, under the influence of Queen Caroline, to have the British Army defend the Neapolitan possessions in Italy. From 1809–13 he was governor of the Leeward Islands. In 1814 he was created Privy Councillor and sent to Madras, where he was governor from 16 September 1814 until 10 June 1820, when he was succeeded by Munro.

5 Munro to Sullivan, 20 January 1815, Gleig, vol. 1, pp. 423–5.

6 Munro to Cumming, 12 January 1815, *ibid.* p. 425.

7 Elliot to W. F. Elphinstone, 25 September 1816, W. F. Elphinstone Papers, I.O. MS Eur. F89, Box 2B. It was also suggested that a 'commission proceeding about the Country as this one will do must give rise to much misconception—there is danger of its even subverting the existing system or at least for a time suspending the operations of the Courts—and unsettling the ideas of the people, now accustomed, and familiar with our Judicial forms'.— 'Remarks on Col. Munro's Commission . . . by a Madras Covenanted Servant' [R. Fullerton], 1 March 1815, I.O. Home Misc., vol. 530, pp. 361–83.

8 R. Fullerton to W. F. Elphinstone, 18 July 1819, W. F. Elphinstone Papers, I.O. MS Eur. F 89, Box 2B.

PAGE 103

1 Government to Munro, 23 September 1814, *SRJ*, vol. 2, p. 291.

2 Munro to Government, 24 December 1814, *SRJ*, vol. 2, pp. 292–6.

3 Minute of Council, 1 March 1815, *SRJ*, vol. 2, pp. 296–302.

4 'Remarks on Col. Munro's Commission . . .' [R. Fullerton], 1 March 1815, I.O. Home Misc., vol. 530, pp. 361–83. See also Minute of Fullerton, 1 January 1816, *SRJ*, vol. 2, pp. 353–75. Fullerton, Robert, writer 1789. Held appointments mainly commercial and judicial, becoming in 1805 general agent for managing the salt monopoly; in 1806 third judge in the northern division of the provincial court; and in 1809 third member of the Board of Trade, and second member of the Council. Fullerton, Munro wrote, was a 'shrewd, intelligent man', but having spent his life in the commercial department except for a few months as circuit judge, he had only a general knowledge of the inhabitants, of local institutions, and of revenue details.—Munro to Sullivan, 20 January 1815, Gleig, vol. 1, pp. 423–5. Time did not soften the verdict: 'a mere Theorist', Munro wrote in 1821, 'and in many things a very extravagant one—and one whose schemes are often dangerous and impracticable. They appear plausible to himself because his want of practical knowledge prevents his seeing the obstacles to their success—and as he is very tenacious of his opinions, he is likely when they happen to be wrong to cause much hindrance to public business in maintaining them.'—Munro to John Ravenshaw, 30 September 1821, Carfrae Papers, I.O. MS Eur. E 225. Elliot reported

that Fullerton was the 'principal opposer' of almost every measure he brought forward; 'I think to the best of my recollection', he wrote in September 1816, 'that almost the only circumstance of any weight during my administration to which he has not given his dissent, was when I proposed to make his Brother a Judge. . . . to the best of my judgment he cannot divest himself of certain local prejudices and perhaps party feelings which prevent him from viewing public matters and interests in their true colours.'—Elliot to W. F. Elphinstone, 25 September 1816, W. F. Elphinstone Papers, I.O. MS Eur. F 89, Box 2B.

5 Stratton, George, writer 1793. Held various revenue appointments from 1799 to 1803 when he was appointed judge of the zillah of Karanguly. In 1806 he was appointed judge of the zillah of Tinnivelly. He was in Britain from 1810 till 1815 when, on his return to India, he was appointed to the Commission. Subsequently he was appointed third member of the Board of Revenue 1819; a member of the Council and president of the Sadr Adalat 1820; and he left Madras in 1824.

6 Minute of Elliot, 3 January 1815, *SRJ*, vol. 2, pp. 271–2.

7 Minute of Council, 1 March 1815, *SRJ*, vol. 2, pp. 296–302.

PAGE 104

1 Munro to Cumming, 1 March 1815, Gleig, vol. 1, pp. 426–9.

2 Commissioners to Government, 28 March 1815, para. 13, *SRJ*, vol. 2, p. 306.

PAGE 105

1 Munro to Government, 24 December 1814, para. 6, *SRJ*, vol. 2, p. 295; also Commissioners to Government, 28 March 1815, para. 21, *ibid.* p. 308.

2 *Ibid.* paras. 2, 20.

3 Munro to Cumming, 9 April 1815, Gleig, vol. 1, pp. 433–4.

4 Minute of Elliot, 13 May 1815, *SRJ*, vol. 2, pp. 309–11; Munro to Cumming, 6 October 1815, Gleig, vol. 1, pp. 440–1.

PAGE 106

1 Munro to Cumming, 1 September 1815, Gleig, vol. 1, pp. 437–40.

PAGE 107

1 Judicial Despatch to Madras, 20 December 1815, *SRJ*, vol. 2, pp. 313–16.

2 Munro to Cumming, 1 March 1815, Gleig, vol. 1, pp. 426–9.

PAGE 108

1 Munro to Cumming, 3 March 1815, Gleig, vol. 1, pp. 429–30.

2 Sullivan, John, writer 1804. In 1814 he was appointed collector of Chingleput; in the following year, collector of Coimbatore; and in 1821 principal collector

and magistrate of Coimbatore. Subsequently he served as senior member of the Board of Revenue 1835, and as a member of the Council 1839. A strong supporter of Munro's views, he wrote *Sketch of the Ryotwar System of Revenue Administration* (London, 1831).

3 Revenue Letter from Madras, 5 January 1816, para. 145, *SRJ*, vol. 1, pp. 710–11.

4 Munro and Sullivan to Government, 26 February 1816, *SRJ*, vol. 1, pp. 712–54.

5 Revenue Despatch to Madras, 22 May 1818, para. 86, *SRJ*, vol. 1, p. 755.

6 Munro to Cumming, 24 September 1816, Gleig, vol. 1, pp. 449–52.

7 It was finally referred to the Board on 12 September 1816. In their comments, 29 December 1817, they had 'no hesitation in recording their opinion, that if complaints were not made to the Courts respecting the abuses in Coimbatore, it is to be attributed to very different causes than the inefficiency of these tribunals'.—MBRC, 29 December 1817, *SRJ*, vol. 1, p. 788. Sullivan criticised this as an 'assertion, unsupported either by reasoning or evidence' (Sullivan to Madras Government, 2 March 1819, *ibid.* p. 808), which criticism appears to be justified.

PAGE 109

1 Minute of Council, 1 March 1815, *SRJ*, vol. 2, pp. 296–302.

2 Commissioners to Government, 15 July 1815, MJC, 19 August 1815.

3 *Ibid.*

4 Minute of Elliot, MJC, 13 October 1815.

5 Extract of proceedings of Sadr Adalat, 2 November 1815, enclosed with Register of Court to Government, 2 November 1815, MJC, 11 November 1815.

6 Extract of proceedings of Sadr Adalat, 14 December 1815, *SRJ*, vol. 2, pp. 317–48. Some months later Fullerton recorded his regret 'that there has not existed that cordial cooperation between [Stratton] and the First and Second Judges . . . the expectation of which led to [his] nomination . . . to the joint office of Judge and Commissioner'.—Minute of Fullerton, 1 March 1816, *SRJ*, vol. 2, pp. 417–20.

PAGE 110

1 Commissioners to Government, 20 April 1816, *SRJ*, vol. 2, pp. 421–33.

2 Minute of Fullerton, 1 March 1816, *SRJ*, vol. 2, pp. 417–20.

PAGE 111

1 Munro to Cumming, 30 April 1816, Gleig, vol. 1, pp. 441–8.

2 Minute of Elliot, 25 April 1816, *SRJ*, vol. 2, p. 435.

3 Commissioners to Government, 15 July 1815, para. 8, MJC, 19 August 1815.

4 *Ibid.* para. 12.

PAGE 112

1 *Ibid.* para. 15.

2 These five regulations became Fort St George Regulations, 1816, IV, V, VI, VII, VIII.

3 Alexander, Robert, writer 1790. Appointed collector in the first division of the Vizagapatam District 1800; judge of the zillah of Vizagapatam 1803; collector in the zillah of Ganjam 1806. In 1808 he became second member of the Board of Revenue, in 1812 senior member, and in 1814 president of the Board and a member of the Council. In 1818 he returned to Britain.

4 Minute of Fullerton, 27 April, Minute of Alexander, 29 April 1816, *SRJ*, vol. 2, pp. 435–6.

5 Minute of Alexander, 17 May 1816, *SRJ*, vol. 2, pp. 440–6.

PAGE 113

1 *Ibid.*

2 Minute of Elliot, 14 May 1816, *SRJ*, vol. 2, pp. 436–7.

3 Judicial Letter from Madras, 26 September 1816, paras. 2–5, *SRJ*, vol. 2, pp. 446–7.

4 The drafts were enclosed with Commissioners to Government, 25 June 1816, MJC, 8 July 1816.

5 Government to Sadr Adalat, 8 July 1816, quoted in proceedings of Sadr Adalat, 29 July 1816, *SRJ*, vol. 2, p. 450.

6 Commissioners to Government, 29 August 1816, *SRJ*, vol. 2, pp. 460–7.

PAGE 114

1 *Ibid.* Fullerton agreed that the commissioners' proposals came 'nearest the expressed object and intention' of the Court of Directors.—Minute of Fullerton, 13 September 1816, *SRJ*, vol. 2, pp. 469–73.

2 Minute of Elliot, 13 September 1816, *SRJ*, vol. 2, p. 469. The regulations became Nos. IX, X, XI of 1816.

3 Regulation XII, 1816.—Commissioners to Government, 4 September 1816, *SRJ*, vol. 2, pp. 467–8.

4 Minutes of Fullerton, 13 September 1816, *SRJ*, vol. 2, pp. 469–74; 17 September 1816, MJC, 20 September 1816. Minute of Alexander, 13 September 1816, *SRJ*, vol. 2, pp. 474–8.

5 Munro to Cumming, 24 September 1816, Gleig, vol. 1, pp. 449–52.

6 Elliot to W. F. Elphinstone, 25 September 1816, W. F. Elphinstone Papers I.O. MS Eur. F 89, Box 2B.

PAGE 115

1 Minute of Elliot, 31 December 1816, *SRJ*, vol. 2, p. 480.

2 Munro to Government, 8 February 1817, *SRJ*, vol. 2, pp. 512–19.

PAGE 116

1 Munro to Government, 26 May 1817, *SRJ*, vol. 2, pp. 529–37.

PAGE 117

1 Munro to Government, 4 July 1817, *SRJ*, vol. 1, pp. 838–58.
2 Fullerton to W. F. Elphinstone, 16 May 1817, W. F. Elphinstone Papers, I.O. MS Eur. F 89, Box 2B.
3 Government to Commissioners, 19 August 1817, MJC, 19 August 1817.

PAGE 118

1 Malcolm to John Adam, 17 February 1818, Gleig, vol. 1, pp. 503–4.
2 Judicial Letter from Madras, 19 March 1818, paras. 24–6, *SRJ*, vol. 2, p. 497. Munro believed that he was regarded at the Presidency as 'a deserter from the Madras Commission' to Elphinstone's.—Munro to M. Elphinstone, 2 September 1818, Mountstuart Elphinstone Papers, I.O. MS Eur. F 88.
3 Munro to Hastings, 12 November 1818, Carfrae Papers, I.O. MS Eur. E 225.

PAGE 119

1 Late Commissioners to Government, 15 October 1818, *SRJ*, vol. 2, pp. 629–36. Stratton had already written a long, factual account of the commission's proceedings.—Stratton to Government, 21 March 1818, *ibid*. pp. 552–99.

2

Years	By the Judge, Assistant Judges, and Registers	By the native Judicatories	Total
1813	4,663	24,888	29,551
1814	5,317	26,717	32,034
1815	7,928	30,687	38,615
1816	7,195	39,714	46,909
1817	4,749	66,302	71,051

—Late Commissioners to Government, 15 October 1818, para. 6. The native judicatories concerned were the former native commissioners, the sadr amins, district munsiffs and district panchayats, and village munsiffs and village panchayats. The increase in the number of suits settled by the last four in 1817 compared with the previous year was:

Years	District Munsiffs	District Panchayats	Village Munsiffs	Village Panchayats
1816	5,133	—	451	95
1817	47,851	112	10,293	250

—Stratton to Government, 13 April 1818, *SRJ*, vol. 2, p. 551 (table 6).

3 Late Commissioners to Government, 15 October 1818, para. 18.
4 *Ibid*. para. 27.

PAGE 120

1 Munro to Hastings, 12 November 1818, Carfrae Papers, I.O. MS Eur. E 225.

PAGE 121

1 Copies of Munro's minutes are in the British Museum, Add. MS 22,071–80. Where they have been printed by Gleig, however, I have given references to that source.

2 Minute of Munro, 12 April 1822, para. 2, Gleig, vol. 2, p. 27.

3 *Ibid*. para. 5, p. 28.

PAGE 122

1 Minute of Munro, 31 December 1824, Gleig, vol. 3, p. 388.

2 Munro to Elphinstone, 26 November 1822, Mountstuart Elphinstone Papers, I.O. MS Eur. F 88.

3 Minute of Munro, 12 April 1822, para. 10, Gleig, vol. 2, p. 31.

PAGE 123

1 *Ibid*. para. 12, pp. 33–4.

2 To Elphinstone he wrote: 'My minute on [the freedom of the press] was but a sketch and it was intended not so much to show how matters actually were as how they might be at a future period if we did not place the Press in this Country under some control' (Munro to Elphinstone, 1 April 1824, Mountstuart Elphinstone Papers, I.O. MS Eur. F 88.); which does suggest a recognition by Munro that he had perhaps let the logic of his argument somewhat outrun what his experience would suggest.

3 Munro's evidence before the House of Commons, 12 April 1813, P.P., 1812–13 (122) VII. 1, p. 131.

4 Munro's evidence, 13 April 1813, *ibid*. p. 143.

5 Minute of Munro, 31 December 1824, Gleig, vol. 3, pp. 360–1. This point is again strongly argued by Munro in a letter to Canning. 'Our present system of Government,' he wrote, 'by excluding all natives from power, and trust, and employment, is much more efficacious in depressing, than all our laws and school-books can do in elevating their character. We are working against our own designs, and we can expect to make no progress while we work with a feeble instrument to improve, and a powerful one to deteriorate. The improvement of the character of a people, and the keeping them, at the same time, in the lowest state of dependence on foreign rulers to which they can be reduced by conquest, are matters quite incompatible with each other.'— Munro to Canning, 30 June 1821, Gleig, vol. 2, p. 58.

6 Charles Grant, *Observations on the State of Society among the Asiatic Subjects of Great Britain, particularly with respect to Morals and on the Means of Improving it. Written chiefly in the Year 1792* (privately printed, 1797).

PAGE 124

1 Munro's evidence before the House of Commons, 12 April 1813, P.P., 1812–13 (122) VII. 1, p. 131. Munro's assertion followed a short disquisition on the variety of qualities which make for a civilised society—a view which Grant could never have accepted. 'With regard to civilization', he told the House, 'I do not exactly understand what is meant by the civilization of the Hindoos; in the higher branches of science, in the knowledge of the theory and practice of good government, and in an education, which, by banishing prejudice and superstition, opens the mind to receive instructions of every kind, from every quarter, they are much inferior to Europeans: but if a good system of agriculture, unrivalled manufacturing skill, a capacity to produce whatever can contribute to convenience or luxury; schools established in every village, for teaching reading, writing and arithmetic; the general practice of hospitality and charity amongst each other; and above all, a treatment of the female sex, full of confidence, respect and delicacy, are among the signs which denote a civilized people, then the Hindoos are not inferior to the nations of Europe'.— Ibid.

2 Charles Grant, *Observations*, p. 71.

3 This paragraph and the one following owe much to Eric Stokes's discussion of the utilitarian and evangelical attitudes to education, *The English Utilitarians and India*, pp. 31–3, 56–7.

4 James Mill, *History of British India*, 2nd ed., vol. 1, p. 247.

5 *Ibid.* vol. 5, pp. 541–2.

PAGE 125

1 Evidence of James Mill before the Select Committee of the House of Commons, P.P., 1831 (320) v. 221, pp. 396–7. 'I consider', Mill stated, 'that the feeling of degradation, from being governed by foreigners, is a feeling altogether European. I believe it has little or no existence in any part of Asia.'— Ibid.

2 Minute of Munro, 31 December 1824, Gleig, vol. 3, p. 362.

PAGE 126

1 'There can be no hope of any great zeal for improvement, when the highest acquirements can lead to nothing beyond some petty office, and can confer neither wealth nor honour. While the prospects of the natives are so bounded, every project for bettering their characters must fail.... This work of improvement, in whatever way it may be attempted, must be slow, but it will be in proportion to the degree of confidence which we repose in them, and in the share which we give them in the administration of public affairs. All that we can give them, without endangering our own ascendancy, should be given.'— Munro to Canning, 30 June 1821, Gleig, vol. 2, p. 58.

2 Minute of Munro, 31 December 1824, Gleig, vol. 3, p. 321.
3 Munro to Sullivan, 24 June 1821, Carfrae MSS, I.O. MS Eur. E 225.
4 *Ibid.*
5 Minute of Munro, 22 January 1821, para. 8, Add. MS 22,077.

PAGE 127
1 *Ibid.* paras. 8–9.
2 Munro to Sullivan, 24 June 1821.

PAGE 128
1 Munro to Elphinstone, 18 June 1818, Mountstuart Elphinstone Papers, I.O. MS Eur. F 88.
2 Munro to Elphinstone, 12 May 1818, *ibid.* Munro wrote again in a similar vein two years later: 'Macdonell has sent you occasionally such of our regulations etc as he thought you would wish to see. But instead of sending you Regulations I would prefer sending you some young men to learn in the Mahratta Provinces what the natives of India are and whether they are likely to be the better of all the dull and heavy Regulations which our supposed wisdom is so fond of imposing upon them. A great proportion of the Madras Districts being under what is called the permanent system affords no proper field for the instruction of young men in a knowledge of the people or of Revenue.'— Munro to Elphinstone, 2 May 1821, *ibid.*
3 Minute of Munro, 29 July 1820, Add. MS 22,076; see also Minute of Munro, 13 May 1825, Add. MS 22,077.
4 Minute of Munro, 8 August 1820, Gleig, vol. 2, p. 15.

PAGE 129
1 Minute of Munro, 31 December 1824, Gleig, vol. 3, p. 320.
2 *Ibid.*

PAGE 130
1 *Ibid.* p. 345.
2 T. E. Colebrooke, *Life of the Honourable Mountstuart Elphinstone*, vol. 2, p. 110.

PAGE 131
1 *Ibid.* p. 292.
2 Munro to his sister Erskine, 1 March 1790, Gleig, vol. 1, pp. 86–7.
3 E.g. see his letter to Lady Munro, 30 May 1821, Gleig, vol. 2, pp. 76–7.
4 Munro to Read, 16 June 1801, Gleig, vol. 3, p. 162.
5 Munro to Canning, 30 June 1821, Gleig, vol. 2, p. 57.

PAGE 132
1 Munro to Canning, 1 May 1823, Gleig, vol. 2, p. 66.
2 Minute of Munro, 31 December 1824, Gleig, vol. 3, p. 379.

PAGE 133
1 Munro to Ravenshaw, 30 September 1821, Carfrae MSS, I.O. MS Eur. E 225.

PAGE 135
1 Minute of Munro, 31 December 1824, Gleig, vol. 3, p. 367.
2 *Ibid.* p. 368.
3 Munro to Ravenshaw, 30 September 1821, Carfrae MSS, I.O. MS Eur. E 225.

PAGE 136
1 *Ibid.*
2 K. N. V. Sastri, in *The Munro System of British Statesmanship in India*, discusses this influence. However, his treatment is so uncritical, and his statements, such as that Munro 'was a practical Burke, and defeated Antichrist in India with moral weapons' (p. LX), are so general (and unsubstantiated) as to render his essay of little value.
3 Kenneth Ballhatchet, *Social Policy and Social Change in Western India 1817–1830*, chaps. 3, 6.
4 Elphinstone to Edward Strachey, 11 March 1822, quoted in Ballhatchet, *ibid.* p. 32.

PAGE 137
1 Percival Spear, *Twilight of the Mughuls*, chap. 5.
2 Eric Stokes, *The English Utilitarians and India*, p. 23.
3 Minute of Bentinck, 10 November 1831, quoted in Stokes, *ibid.* p. 165.

PAGE 138
1 Percival Spear, *India, Pakistan and the West*, p. 124.

GLOSSARY

adalat, adawlut	law court
amildar	district officer
bazar	retail daily market, shopping centre
Brahmin, Brahman	priest
circar	*see* sarkar
curnum	*see* karnam
cutcherry	*see* kachahri
daroga, darogha	superintendent or overseer
enam, enaum	*see* inam
fasli, fusly	of or belonging to a harvest
ghat, ghaut	mountains, mountain pass
gour	head man of a village
havelly	(in Madras) lands under the immediate management of government
inam, enam, enaum	rent-free land
jagir, jageer	assignment of land and its rent, with or without conditions of service
jama, jumma	the total demand for revenue of all kinds payable by a cultivator
kachahri, cutcherry	government office
karnam, curnum	village registrar and accountant
lakh, lack	one hundred thousand
mirasdar	the holder of permanent proprietary rights in land
munsiff, moonsiff	lit. A just and equitable man. Native justice or judge with limited powers
panchayat, punchayet	committee, traditionally of five members, to whom a cause may be referred for investigation and decision
patel, potail	village headman
patta, puttah, potta	revenue certificate
peshkash, peshcush	a present, particularly to government, in consideration of an appointment, or as an acknowledgement for any tenure, e.g. the tribute paid by the poligars to government
poligar	military chieftain
potail	*see* patel
punchayet	*see* panchayat

172

puttah, potta	*see* patta
ryot, rayet, raiyat	peasant
ryotwari settlement	revenue settlement between government and peasant without intermediaries
Sadr Adalat, Sudder Adawlut	supreme court of the Presidency
sanad, sunnud	a patent, charter, or written authority for holding either land or office
sarishtadar, sheristadar	record keeper
sarkar, sircar	a Mughul district. Used as a synonym for government
sastras	medieval Hindu texts giving instruction in religious and legal questions
Sudder Adawlut	*see* Sadr Adalat
sunnud	*see* sanad
tahsildar	a native collector of a district acting under a European collector or a zamindar
tank	reservoir
thanadar	deputy inspector of police
vakil, vackeel	agent, pleader, or advocate
zamindar, zemindar	landholder, district official
zamindari settlement	revenue settlement between government and (substantial) landholder
zillah	a district

BIBLIOGRAPHY

This study is based primarily on Munro's official letters and reports among the collection of manuscript records in the India Office Library and Record Department, Commonwealth Relations Office, London. I was unable to locate the private papers of Munro, used by his biographer, the Rev. G. R. Gleig, for three volumes published in 1830, if indeed these papers remained as one collection. It seems unlikely that Munro's papers were ever in the possession of his widow and sons after his death. The family house, near Forfar in Scotland, was pulled down by the present baronet, Sir Torquil Munro, and the library sold. Sir Torquil certainly has no papers of his great-grandfather in his possession; nor, apparently, have any other members of the family. The National Register of Archives has no record of any Munro material. While Gleig quotes extensively from private correspondence, and also makes some use of published official documents, it seems doubtful whether there ever was any comprehensive collection of Munro papers, as was the case with some of his contemporaries. Among the Wellesley Papers in the British Museum is one volume [Add. MS 13,679] listed as 'Letters, Papers and Reports of Colonel Munro chiefly relating to Canara and the Ceded Districts 1799–1805'. In the front of the volume is a note reading: 'Col Munro has the pleasure of sending Mr Campbell a Book containing some documents relating to Canara and the Ceded Districts—Some papers of a private correspondence between Lord Wm Bentinck—Mr Petrie and Col Munro have by accident been bound up with them—Col Munro will endeavour to find some more papers on the same subject and send them to Mr Campbell.' Such generosity to his friends clearly was to provide difficulties for future students of Munro's career. At this moment that is about as far as one can get with the question of 'the Munro papers', and it is obviously not very far.

Abbreviations used in the text or notes are shown in square brackets

I. MANUSCRIPT SOURCES

A. British Museum, London

Warren Hastings' Papers in Additional Manuscripts [Hastings Papers].
The Minutes of Sir Thomas Munro as Governor of Madras, in Additional Manuscripts [Munro's Minutes].
The Marquess of Wellesley's Papers in Additional Manuscripts [Wellesley Papers].

B. *India Office Library and Record Department, Commonwealth Relations Office, London*

Appendix to Court Minutes.
Correspondence Reports. (Reports and resolutions of the Correspondence Committee.)
Court Minutes.
Despatches to Madras (original drafts).
Draft Despatches (to Madras) submitted by the Court to the Board of Control.
European Manuscripts.
    (i) Carfrae MSS, MS Eur. E 183, E 184, E 225.
    (ii) Erskine MSS, MS Eur. D 31, D 32.
    (iii) Mountstuart Elphinstone Papers, MS Eur. F 88.
    (iv) William Fullarton Elphinstone Papers, MS Eur. F 89.
Home Miscellaneous Series.
    (i) James Cumming's Papers. Home Misc. vols. 525–31, 686, 692–4.
    (ii) Vols. 462, 486.
Judicial Despatches to Madras.
Judicial Letters from Madras.
Letters from the Board of Control to the East India Company.
Letters from the East India Company to the Board of Control.
Madras Board of Revenue Consultations/Proceedings [MBRC].
Madras Consultations/Proceedings of the Special Commission for the Permanent Settlement.
Madras Judicial Consultations/Proceedings [MJC].
Madras Political Consultations/Proceedings [MPC].
Madras Revenue Consultations/Proceedings [MRC].
Madras Secret Consultations/Proceedings [MSC].
Memoranda of the Correspondence Committee.
Minutes of the Board of Control.
Minutes of the Secret Committee of Correspondence.
Miscellaneous Letters Received (by the Court of Directors).
Personal Records.
Revenue Despatches to Madras.
Revenue Letters from Madras.

C. *Madras Record Office*

Public Department: Sundries
    121.   Letters and Reports of Thomas Munro, Salem District, 1792–1799.
    122.   Copies of Thomas Munro's minutes, Ceded Districts, 1805–1806.

123-8. Rough records of Thomas Munro, Principal Collector of Bellamy, 1800–1807.

129. Copies of Thomas Munro's minutes, 1821–1826.

D. *National Library of Scotland, Edinburgh*

Memoir by Munro on the Madras Judicial System, MS 12.

E. *Nottingham University Library*

Lord William Cavendish Bentinck's Papers in the Portland Collection [Bentinck Papers].

F. *John Rylands Library, Manchester*

Papers of Henry Dundas, 1st Viscount Melville, and Robert Dundas, 2nd Viscount Melville [Melville Papers].

2. PRINTED PRIMARY SOURCES: OFFICIAL

Baramahal Records, 13 vols., Madras, 1907–20 [*B.R.*].

Fort St George Regulations.

Madras Record Office: Printed Selections from District Records

Bellary District (vols. 72, 76, 77, 79).

South Kanara District (vol. 174).

Parliamentary Debates from the year 1803 . . . forming a continuation of the work entitled 'The Parliamentary History of England from the earliest period to the year 1803'. Published under the superintendence of T. C. Hansard, 22 November 1803–28 February 1820. 41 vols., London [Hansard].

Parliamentary Papers

1812   *The Fifth Report from the Select Committee on the Affairs of the East India Company. Ordered by the House of Commons to be printed, 28 July 1812.* 1812 (377) VII. 1 [*Fifth Report*].

1812–13 *Minutes of Evidence taken before the Committee of the whole House on the affairs of the East India Company* [P.P., 1812–13 (122) VII. 1].

1831   *Minutes of Evidence taken before the Select Committee on the affairs of the East India Company* [P.P., 1831 (320) V. 221].

1831–2 *Minutes of Evidence taken before the Select Committee on the affairs of the East India Company.*

   I. *Public* [P.P., 1831–2 (735—I) IX. 1].

   III. *Revenue* [P.P., 1831–2 (735—III) XI. 1].

   IV. *Judicial* [P.P., 1831–2 (735—IV) XII. 1].

Selection of Papers from the Records at the East-India House Relating to the Revenue, Police, and Civil and Criminal Justice under the Company's Governments in India, 4 vols., London, 1820–6 [*SRJ*].

3. PRINTED PRIMARY SOURCES: UNOFFICIAL

Brief Notice of the Services of Mr Cumming, Late Head of the Revenue and Judicial Departments in the Office of the Right Honourable the Board of Commissioners for the Affairs of India, London, 1824 [*Brief Notice of the Services of Mr Cumming*].

Cornwallis, Charles, Marquess Cornwallis. *Correspondence*, edited by Charles Ross. 3 vols., 2nd ed., London, 1859.

East-India Register.

Grant, Charles. *Observations on the State of Society among the Asiatic Subjects of Great Britain, particularly with respect to Morals and on the Means of Improving it. Written chiefly in the year 1792*. London, 1797 (privately printed).

Munro. Major General Sir Thomas Munro Bart., K.C.B. Governor of Madras. *Selections from his Minutes and other Official writings*, edited by Sir Alexander J. Arbuthnot. 2 vols., London, 1881.

Sajunlal, K. 'A few unpublished letters of Sir Thomas Munro', in *Indian Historical Records Commission Proceedings*, vol. XXXI, part 2, 1955. Printed correspondence of Munro.

Sastri, K. N. Venkatasubba. 'More Light on Sir Thomas Munro', in *Indian Historical Records Commission Proceedings*, vol. XIV, 1937. Printed correspondence of Munro.

[Sullivan, J.] *Sketch of the Ryotwar System of Revenue Administration*. London, 1831.

Wellesley. Richard Colley, Marquess Wellesley. *The Despatches, Minutes and Correspondence of the Marquess Wellesley during his administration in India*, edited by R. Montgomery Martin. 5 vols., London, 1836–7.

Wellington. Arthur Wellesley, Duke of Wellington. *The Despatches of . . . the Duke of Wellington . . . during his various campaigns in India, Denmark, Portugal, Spain, the Low Countries and France from 1799 to 1818*, compiled . . . by Lieut.-Colonel Gurwood. 13 vols., London, 1834–9.

Wellington. Arthur Wellesley, Duke of Wellington. *Supplementary despatches, correspondence and memoranda of . . . Arthur Duke of Wellington*, edited by his son, the Duke of Wellington. 15 vols., London, 1858–72.

Wilks, Mark. *Historical Sketches of the South of India*. 3 vols., London, 1810–14.

4. SECONDARY WORKS

Aspinall, A. *Cornwallis in Bengal*. Manchester, 1931.

Auber, Peter. *Rise and Progress of the British Power in India*. 2 vols., London, 1837.

Baden-Powell, B. H. *The Indian Village Community*. London, 1896.

Baden-Powell, B. H. *The Land Systems of British India*. 3 vols., Oxford, 1892.

Baliga, B. S. 'Home Government and the end of the policy of Permanent Settlement in Madras, 1802 to 1818', in *Indian Historical Records Commission Proceedings*, vol. XIX, 1942.

Baliga, B. S. 'The influence of the Home Government on land revenue and judicial administration in the Presidency of Fort William in Bengal from 1807 to 1822.' Unpublished Ph.D. thesis, University of London, 1933.

Baliga, B. S. 'Village Settlement of Land Revenue in Madras, 1807–22', in *Indian Historical Records Commission Proceedings*, vol. XXI, 1944.

Ballhatchet, Kenneth. *Social Policy and Social Change in Western India 1817–1830*. London, 1957.

Ballhatchet, Kenneth. 'The Authors of the Fifth Report of 1812', in *Notes and Queries*, vol. CCII, 1957.

Basham, A. L. *The Wonder that was India*. London, 1954.

Bradshaw, John. *Sir Thomas Munro*. Oxford, 1906.

The Cambridge History of India, vol. 5. Cambridge, 1932.

Chaudhuri, S. B. *Civil Disturbances during the British Rule in India, 1765–1857*, Calcutta, 1955.

Colebrooke, Sir T. E. *Life of the Honourable Mountstuart Elphinstone*. 2 vols., London, 1884.

Dutt, Romesh Chunder. *The Economic History of India under Early British Rule. From the Rise of British Power in 1757 to the Accession of Queen Victoria in 1837*. 2nd ed., London, 1906.

Dykes, James William Ballantyne. *Salem, an Indian Collectorate*. London, 1853 [Dykes, *Salem*].

Embree, Ainslie. *Charles Grant and British Rule in India*. London, 1962.

Gleig, The Rev. G. R. *The Life of Major General Sir Thomas Munro, Bart. and K.C.B. Late Governor of Madras*. 3 vols., London, 1830. Includes a considerable amount of Munro's correspondence [Gleig].

Gopal, S. *The Permanent Settlement in Bengal and its Results*. London, 1949.

Gribble, J. D. B. *Manual of the District of Cuddapah*. Madras, 1875.

Kaye, Sir John William, *The Administration of the East India Company: a history of Indian Progress*. London, 1953.

Kaye, Sir John William. *The Life and Correspondence of Charles, Lord Metcalfe*. 2 vols., 2nd ed., London, 1854.

Kaye, Sir John William. *The Life and Correspondence of Major General Sir John Malcolm*. 2 vols., London, 1856.

Kelsall, John. *Manual of the Bellary District*. Madras, 1872.

Krishnaswami, P. R. *Tom Munro Saheb Governor of Madras: a Portrait with a selection of his letters*. Madras, 1947.

'The Land Revenue of Madras', in *Calcutta Review*, vol. XVII, 1853.

Le Fanu, H. *A Manual of the Salem District in the Presidency of Madras.* 2 vols., Madras, 1826.

Malcolm, Sir John. *The Political History of India from 1784 to 1823.* 2 vols., London, 1826.

Matthai, John. *Village Government in British India.* London, 1915.

Mill, James. *The History of British India.* 6 vols., 2nd ed., London, 1802.

Misra, B. B. *The Central Administration of the East India Company 1773–1834.* Manchester, 1959.

Morris, Henry. *The Life of Charles Grant.* London, 1904.

Mukherjee, Nilmani. *The Ryotwari System in Madras 1792–1827.* Calcutta, 1962.

Philips, C. H. *The East India Company, 1792–1843.* Manchester, 1940.

Roberts, P. E. *India under Wellesley.* London, 1929.

Raju, A. Sarada. *Economic Conditions in the Madras Presidency 1800–1850.* Madras, 1941.

Ruthnaswamy, M. *Some Influences that made the British Administrative System in India.* London, 1939.

Sastri, K. N. Venkatasubba. *The Munro System of British Statesmanship in India.* Mysore, 1939.

Sinha, J. C. 'Economic Conditions of the Ceded Districts (1800–1807)', in *Indian Historical Records Commission Proceedings*, vol. XVII, 1939.

'Sir Thomas Munro and the Land Tax', in *Calcutta Review*, vol. XV, 1851.

Spear, Percival. *Twilight of the Mughuls.* Cambridge, 1951.

Srinivasachariar, C. S. 'The Settlement of Baramahal and Salem from the Records', in *Journal of Indian History*, vol. IV, part 1, 1926.

Stokes, Eric. *The English Utilitarians and India.* Oxford, 1959.

Thompson, Edward. *The Making of the Indian Princes.* London, 1943.

Thornton, Edward. *The History of the British Empire in India.* 6 vols., London, 1841.

Wilson, H. H. *History of British India from 1805 to 1835.* 3 vols., London, 1838.

Wright, H. R. C. 'Some Aspects of the Permanent Settlement in Bengal', in *Economic History Review*, 2nd Series, vol. VII, no. 2, 1954.

Wright, H. R. C. *East-Indian Economic Problems of the Age of Cornwallis and Raffles.* London, 1961.

INDEX

INDEX

Poligars (*cont.*)
  Vithal, 39–40
Private property in land, 74
  granted by Cornwallis to zamindars, 5
  in Kanara, 48, 53–4
  unknown in Ceded Districts, 69, 79–80

Rao, Hunamant, 136
Rao, Lakshman, 136
Ravenshaw, John, 53, 55, 149
Read, Alexander
  appointed in charge of Baramahal, 14
  early career and character, 14–15
  ideas on judicial system, 31–2
  relations with Board of Revenue, 30–1
  rules for revenue settlement, 23–4
Rickards, Robert, 97, 161
  on effects of Bengal system, 95–6
Ripaud, 35
Ryotwari settlement: developed in Madras,
  8–9
  in Baramahal: accepted by Munro,
  25–30; disapproved by Board of
  Revenue, 30–1; principles developed
  by Read, 23–4
  in Ceded Districts: advocated by
  Munro, 79–84; Munro's method of
  settlement, 70–1
  ordered in Madras, 93
  seen by Munro as natural state of country,
  129–30
  supported by Cumming, 89–92

Sadr Adalat, 113
  opposes regulations of Judicial Commission, 109–10

Separation of Powers: opposed by Munro,
  32–3, 75
  supported by Fullerton, 103, 114
  Wellesley's enthusiasm for, 74
Small landholders, Munro's preference
  for, 8, 28, 51–2
Stodart, Alexander, 55, 150
Stratton, George, 164
  appointed to Commission for revision
  of Madras Judicial system, 103
Sullivan, John, 93
Sullivan, John, 108, 164–5
Survey
  in Ceded Districts, 71–2
  in Kanara, 50

Tanjore, position of patels, 115
Thackeray, William, 55, 150
  memoir on ryotwari settlement, 78
Thornton, Henry, defends Cornwallis
  system, 96–7
Tipu
  defeated by Cornwallis, 12
  defeated by Wellesley, 36
  settlement of Kanara, 47–9

Utilitarians, administrative debt to Munro,
  137

Vijayanagar, settlement of Kanara, 47–8
Village settlement, tried in Madras, 84–6

Webbe, Josiah, 64, 150
Wellesley, Marquis, 6–7
  queries on judicial system, 94–5
Wellesley, Arthur, 43

Zamindars, recognised by Cornwallis as
  proprietors of the soil, 5